from Deborah to Esther

from Deborah to Esther

sexual politics IN THE HEBREW BIBLE

Lillian R. Klein

FORTRESS PRESS

MINNEAPOLIS

FROM DEBORAH TO ESTHER
Sexual Politics in the Hebrew Bible

Cover image: Double-headed goat or horse motif pendant on a necklace of irregular carnelian beads, c. 2000 B.C.E. Found in the cemetery at Dhaiyah, Ras al-Khaimah, United Arab Emirates. Ras al-Khaimah Museum. Copyright Werner Forman/Art Resource, N.Y. Used by permission.
Cover and book design: Ann Delgehausen
Author photo: Connie Reider, Bethesda, Maryland

ISBN 0-8006-3592-2

The paper used in this publication meets the minimum requirements of American National Standard for Information Sciences—Permanence of Paper for Printed Library Materials, ANSI Z329.48-1984.

Manufactured in the U.S.A.
07   06   05   04   03   1   2   3   4   5   6   7   8   9   10

A good man, who can find?
  He is far more precious than pearls
The heart of his wife trusts in him.

—*pace* Proverbs 31:10-11

אשׁ־חיל מי ימצא ורחוק מפנינם מכרו
בטח בו לב אשתו

THIS BOOK IS DEDICATED TO A MAN WHO IS TRULY GOOD

My beloved husband, Seymour S. Abensohn

Contents

Preface

*D*espite a well-publicized suggestion that one book of the Bible reflects a woman's point of view and was, in fact, written by a woman;[1] and the possibility that the Song of Songs reflects female voices,[2] the essays of this book are based on a less radical assumption: that most biblical texts are texts created by educated men in positions of authority and power. The texts reflect various sources of that power—primarily the realms of monarchy, priest and prophet. Each of these points of view encompasses an entire "worldview" and determines the character and actions of the individuals involved in a specific narrative. However, regardless of the disparity in sources of power, there is surprising agreement among the stories about the roles of females. Males may have disputed with one another about male power, but they were largely in agreement about control of females.

It seems safe to conclude that, in general, constraints on women are created by physically dominant males. Physical dominance leads, sooner or later, to psychological dominance, whereby the woman accepts her place as dominated and cooperates in it. Female acceptance of male dominance results in social and cultural subservience, and "might" has indeed made "right." One significant aspect of male control of females is by restriction of the women to nonpublic areas, primarily the home, by invoking female "shame" and male "honor." The women cooperate in protecting their males' (fathers/husbands) honor by demonstrating proper "shame" in their modest behavior and remaining out of the sight of other, non-related males. Out of the world of history, of events in places of power, females are, in effect, "shamed" into nonexistence in much of biblical literature: many have no names, no genealogy, and are often not even mentioned as existent (e.g., daughters).

Biblical literature describes such a culture, one in which males are dominant and females largely accept their position as subservient. It is the exceptions, the women whose stories are told—whether peripherally or centrally—that we will address. In each of these stories, variations on constraints of females reveals the particular worldview of the author/redactor. Keeping in mind that men wrote these stories, how did these women escape oblivion? Was the memory of a female figure too strong in tradition? Were female actions depicted to contrast with those of males? Were females used as positive/negative examples? Or, reversing the perspective, what do these images of women say about the males who wrote them?

Students of biblical literature are enriched by addressing as many perspectives of the narratives as possible. Gender perspectives of biblical literature are relevant to males as well as females: they invite males to explore their own gendered social attitudes through the distance of time and the richness of the narratives. Feminist perspectives are perhaps most important to women: in addition to offering a place in the text and exploration of female-gendered social attitudes, they also invite consideration of the male need to exercise control, particularly of females, disclosed in the narratives and the possible implications of that need. Is there a female counterpart to that masculine control in the text? In contemporary experience?

I wish to note here that the text on which these essays are based is the Masoretic text of the Hebrew Bible, which differs in sequence and in points of translation from the English Old Testament.[3] Accordingly, the first five books of the Bible are referred to as the Torah, not the Pentateuch. The translations are my own, although I have occasionally used *JPS Hebrew-English Tanakh* (Philadelphia: The Jewish Publication Society, 1999) and *The New Oxford Annotated Bible*, RSV (Oxford: Oxford University Press, 1977) as points of reference.

These essays evolved from a chance meeting—at an outdoor patio table, under a broad umbrella shading the blazing midday heat—in Germany. In 1992, I was living and teaching in Munich; I had gone to Bendorf for the annual Jewish-Christian Bible Week of the Leo Baeck College in collaboration with the Hedwig Dransfeld-Haus, and to hear the renowned feminist author, Professor Athalya Brenner, speak on that occasion. Between workshops and lectures, I happened to see Dr. Brenner on the patio and she invited me to join her at her table for lunch. We had seen one another, in passing, at Annual Meetings of the Society of Biblical Literature, but had never had an opportunity to talk. I had already been impressed by her lecture the evening before and was delighted to make a closer acquaintance; when she invited me to submit articles to the *Feminist Companion to the Bible* (Sheffield: Sheffield Academic, 1993–2001) she was editing, I readily agreed. From that chance meeting has come not only this series of essays, most of which were printed in various volumes of the *Feminist Companion*, but an enduring and endearing friendship. I count Athalya Brenner as my editor of many years, among my closest friends, and as a woman for whom I have profound respect and admiration: *ahuva v'shalom*.

Any book stands of the shoulders of many sources; I shall restrict myself to those who were most directly involved. First of all, I wish to thank Athalya Brenner, for all of the reasons mentioned above, and more. I also wish to thank Yocheved Karlin, who patiently helped me with transliteration of the Hebrew; and Michael West and K. C. Hanson, my enthusiastic and supportive editors at Fortress Press. I add a special note of thanks to Philip Davies and other friends at Sheffield Academic Press for years of friendly collaboration and for generously releasing these essays for publication. To my husband, Seymour S. Abensohn, who demonstrates none of the need for masculine domination evident in biblical literature and, in fact, enthusiastically supports my independent activity in realms largely foreign to him, I offer my love and profound appreciation.

Introduction

As a female, girl, and woman, I have had difficulty relating to biblical narratives.[1] The paradigm roles of the male protagonists were always clear at one level: obedience to God and diligence, with emphasis shifting between the two. Women's roles were similar, only the obedience required was to her human counterpart who may—or may not—have deserved her subservience. The women were usually presented as peripheral to a narrative, perhaps reproductive necessities, sometimes difficult and potentially dangerous, occasionally central, but almost always with male controls. Women were often nameless, mostly without genealogies, which effectively rendered them without existence. Once they had accomplished their narrative "mission," women tended to disappear from the text without further ado. It is rare indeed to hear of a woman's death.[2] True, women were occasionally honored, but they were marginalized at the same time; and rivalry among women received a different kind of attention than rivalry among men. As a biblical and literary scholar functioning in the contemporary world, I entertained the idea that a closer analysis of biblical texts would not only help me find my place in biblical narratives but also clarify my place in the "sexual politics" of daily life: the give and take within a society that reflects gender valuation and defines gender roles.

It seems safe to infer that women were found in the fringes of most—but not all—narratives because it reflects their role in the social world of the narrative. The laws of Torah do not prescribe such limitations except in periods associated with menstruation, sexual activity and childbirth (e.g., Lev 12:6; 15:19).[3] Men are similarly "unclean" after sexual intercourse (Lev 15:16) and other, nonsexual conditions. The sexual activity of women is, like that of men, restricted to marital relationships; men are further cautioned from incestuous relationships (Lev 21:10-21; Num 5:11-31.) The Torah makes little mention of laws restricting females in activity, but the narratives of Torah do depict females, including wives, restricted to minor appearances and being regarded as sexual objects, exchanged like objects by males (Gen 20:2-7). It is the narratives, not the laws, that establish the roles of women in various temporal phases of biblical literature. Indeed, in Proverbs 31, an ideal Israelite woman is shown to be active and commanding in the marketplace as well as in the home: this woman purchases property and manages finances while her husband apparently has nothing to do but to "sit among the elders of the land at the gates" (31:28). The unusual freedom and authority granted this ideal woman may be theoretical as well as ideal; at best they reflect a specific and limited position in the long history reflected in biblical narrative. Yet even this poetic paean to the ideal housewife is constrained between warnings to males, preceding and following the lines of tribute, about the dangers of femmes fatales: "Give not your strength to women, your ways to those who destroy kings" (31:3). "Charm is deceitful, and beauty is vain" (31:30).

In the narratives, the world outside the home was the domain of men; within the home, the women had more authority: essentially, authority over their children. Such social structures are to be found to this day among some Middle Eastern religious groups, and they are a valuable resource for studying the social milieu of the Hebrew Bible.[4] Then as now, women restricted to the home have limited if any education and little exposure; as a result, they have little opportunity to celebrate or record their relatively uneventful lives. The men were more likely to lead lives of power; and biblical narratives describe male control or control desired over one another and over females, and the struggles to achieve and maintain that power.

When female figures are introduced into male-dominant narratives, they may provide peripheral information about the male protagonist and the prevalent sexual politics of that narrative period.

However, the modern reader must disabuse him/herself of the idea of equality of the sexes (a relatively modern concept and one that has yet to achieve full realization). When angels visit Abraham and predict the birth of a son to the aging couple, they react very differently indeed to similar responses from husband and wife. Both laugh when they hear this unexpected news (Gen 17:17; 18:12), but only Sarah is rebuked for laughing . . . and laughing "to herself." Intimidated, she denies laughing and is again repudiated. This slight passage indicates how women may be oppressed and made fearful by strangers and by husbands who do nothing to protect them, how women are shown to resort to lying to protect themselves, how men easily bond to maintain control over women at every turn.

As societies develop and change so does the role of women, and biblical narratives reveal subtle periodization of women's roles. An obvious fluctuation is the role of foreign women among the tribes: the story of Ruth celebrates full acceptance of Ruth, a Moabite woman,[5] whereas the narrative of Dinah (Genesis 34) describes the treacherous murder of the whole town of Shechem because a foreigner had dared to love a daughter of Israel. It is worth noting that the Israelite males are rebuked time and time again for taking foreign wives at various phases—which indicates that the practice was fairly common; but a singular instance where an Israelite female is desired by a foreign male is emphatically rejected by wholesale murder.

Biblical narratives suggest social and textual boundaries for interaction between the sexes. The value ascribed to each of the genders is a case in point. There is practically no mention of daughters in biblical narratives; only the birth of sons is noted unless and until a daughter becomes a focal point, for example, Dinah (Gen 30:21; 34). As mentioned, females are frequently unnamed whereas their male counterparts have names and often genealogies. Although this device is used to ironic effect in the story of Manoah and his wife (Judg 13:2-20),[6] the major implication is the lack of value ascribed to females in the dominant culture. Devaluation is yet another means of control.[7]

Rivalry is another aspect that seems to be gender-specific. When males combat for power, it is often viewed as heroic; when women desire the same, within their constrained realm, they are made to seem petty. The power that women desire is usually limited to that associated with motherhood. A married woman who does not bear a child suffers a severe loss in social status and even her livelihood may be a fragile entity. That women manipulate and maneuver in order to assure themselves of childbirth is consistent with the social reality. Motherhood is a vital issue for women in this culture.

Some narratives disclose males' wishful thinking and projection in stories about women. Rivalry among females, mentioned above, shows women fighting among themselves for the love of a man and even trading a night of copulation for the promise of pregnancy (Gen 30:1-24). Of course female rivalry over a man is very flattering to the male ego and sense of power. It is not surprising that rivalry among women was encouraged or at least projected as normal in these stories. Married biblical women are portrayed as so zealous of bearing children that they seem never to "have a headache." Is this social oppression or male fantasy? Biblical men are never infertile, either; that problem always resides with the woman, sometimes because yet another male figure, God, has "closed up her womb." One narrative suggests the ultimate male punishment of a wife: refusal to cohabit so that she cannot bear children (Michal, in 2 Sam 6:23).[8] Even the daughter of a king can be rendered powerless and insignificant by a man. And if women act unjustly among themselves, abusing power given to them, as in the Sarah and Hagar narrative, surely a male divine figure will come along to justify the outcome of the situation (Gen 16:1-15).

Several narratives do have female protagonists, with males playing "background" roles. Once again, the story of Ruth is a good example. Naomi and Ruth do determine the actions of the narrative, but they clearly act within the parameters of a male-determinant society. They know how to manipulate in order to achieve their goals, and manipulation is a power associated with women. In this narrative, even sexual manipulation by a woman is not condemned, presumably because the objective is fertility (and implicit economic security), not personal pleasure or power. Generally, biblical narratives repudiate a woman's exerting control, but she may manipulate in order to achieve specific and limited goals, so long as these are goals valued by the larger society. Bathsheba, as we will see, is another mistress of balancing these elements.

Female sexuality is an interesting variable. Wives and mothers are not attributed sexuality; and women who are clearly enticing to males are usually regarded as extremely dangerous, inherently evil. Women are shown to use their sexuality as a manipulative tool to various effects (Ruth 3:7; Judges 16); in general, males condemn female sexuality. In fact, the very emphasis put on male control of female sexuality invites further consideration of the threat implicit in female sexuality. The most obvious need to control female sexuality is based on the problem of identifying the father of the woman's child, but is there more? Female sexuality may assert a kind of control: women have something they can give—or deny—to men. Men want to desire women, but they do not want to be denied by women. Women who are independent in their sexuality are exerting control over men and are therefore potentially dangerous, even evil.

A few women transgress these constraints, some successfully, some not. The following chapters explore images of women who have been traditionally and relatively neglected by commentary as well as more popular female characters, here viewed through literary and other lenses. As a scholar of biblical texts, my first avenue of approach to a text is to invoke the entire array of literary-critical techniques, from classical to contemporary. I have found that "point of view" is extremely valuable for both narrative and individual speakers, and that it is used in a surprisingly modern way in these ancient texts. In the Book of Judges, for instance, the exposition (chs. 1–2) is presented twice, in succession, from divine and human points of view.[9] (I had previously thought that was a twentieth-century innovation.) A modern literary technique, structural analysis, has informed much of my work. But I have also drawn from contemporary sociological and psychological approaches to understand implicit as well as explicit messages in the text. After all, a biblical text is not only an expression of religious issues: it involves the breadth of human experience and is transmitted in a literary form. As techniques for analysis of human experience become available, they must be absorbed into the methodology of the literary critic.

The text determines the methodology, not vice versa. Just as some texts are informed by structure or character and others by psychological or sociological parameters, each must be analyzed to determine which method or methods will be most rewarding in exposition of the subtext. And because these texts are based on the fullness of human nature, its failures and its attributes, there is nothing inherently contradictory to theology in a multivalent approach to study of the texts.[10]

I did not approach these essays about biblical women with any idea of an overriding purpose; I merely sought to explore each narrative individually. However, as I think about them in retrospect, I have become aware of several dominant aspects. The first is the preoccupation with power and control, already mentioned. Biblical narratives are largely about power struggles, and modern writing—from newspaper articles to novels—is about power struggles: between the sexes, among men or women and between generations. The nature of the power and the struggle may have changed, but the human appetite for power apparently remains constant.

Another motif I discovered in reading these biblical narratives is more surprising: male fear of female power. Female sexuality is dangerous: "Give not your strength to women, your ways to those who destroy kings" (Prov 31:3). Note that even kings, those males with the utmost human power, are also subject to infatuation with "a loose woman, and embrace the bosom of an adventuress" (Prov 5:20). The power of female sexuality is potentially greater than that of the king. As a further insult to masculine dominance, female reproductive power totally defies male control. There is no way males can bear children, though various texts allude to attempts. In the creation stories, after all, God creates Adam without the help of a woman, and Eve is created out of Adam, again without a woman.[11] Such masculine anxieties about women suggest a source of textual repression of female characters. The chapter about Job will address this issue.

The relevance of these narrated male fears of female power to the modern situation is difficult to assess: the situation of women has changed dramatically with the advent of birth control. At present, women can be much more in control of their lives than they ever were. Equality of the sexes is not yet a reality in terms of equal pay for equal work in many fields, but significant changes in that direction have been made. In Western societies, women may be largely independent of men for their livelihood and even for child-bearing: semen can be obtained through artificial insemination without a woman's even meeting the "father" of her child. Males, on the other hand, have not yet achieved independence of females as bearers of children, although cloning may indeed make female presence as unnecessary as that of the male. How these changes are already affecting male consciousness is a factor we should take into consideration, especially in light of the ancient anxieties revealed in these texts.

How does AI serve this purpose?

We may ask what it is that a hypothetical male of biblical narrative desires to find in a hypothetically ideal female. With all the emphasis on control, one might assume that a passive, sexually compliant female would be the ideal mate. However, biblical texts repeatedly contradict this idea: women who are intelligent and display initiative are emphasized as desirable. Beauty is certainly valued, as is sexual attractiveness, but they are not alluded to as often as intelligence and initiative. Fertility is a critical matter, although some biblical marriages are successful for many years, and the wife may be expressly loved, without childbearing (e.g., Sarah, Rachel). The role of a desirable woman is thus extremely difficult: she should be intelligent, which makes the possibility of independent thinking more likely, but she must also restrict her actions to the constraints of the patriarchal mores. Because of the inaccessibility of education, an intelligent woman had to learn independently, possibly deviously. She should be faithful to the one God of her fathers and husband, albeit without being taught anything except, possibly, ritual—passed from mother to daughter. She should be beautiful or at least sexually attractive; she should know how to stimulate and manipulate her husband with sexual provocation in order to realize her own desires, but that sexuality must be invisible to all but her husband. She should be fertile, bearing sons. For the husband, control and power over passive, unstimulating females capable only of reproducing and doing household chores seems to be not especially gratifying. The potential of resistance, of deviance, of engagement, of stimulation—even of loss—gives significance to power. Should a woman succeed in mastering and surpassing these constraints, she might be able to leave her story to posterity—even though told through male perception. What an exciting paradox or contradiction in terms!

These narratives about how women have coped with social constraints are as varied as life itself. Each story describes different circumstances and different responses, often buried in the subtext rather than explicit in the overtly male-oriented narrative. These narratives of females coping with male-imposed constraints, of living meaningful lives within social boundaries or by extending those boundaries, are still inherently relevant to contemporary life.

Wives and Daughters
in the Book of Judges

A Spectrum of Female Characters
in the Book of Judges

Some of the most unforgettable females of the Hebrew Bible make their appearances in the Book of Judges, and several have individually been subject to scrutiny;[1] however, to my knowledge, an overall view of the range and function of these characters has never been addressed. When we realize that eleven fully differentiated females take part in various narrative segments, even though three main-judge narratives—Ehud, Gideon, and Abimelech—do not dramatize any female characters, we recognize that an unusual density and variety of women appear in these pages. In order to indicate the range of roles suggested for the female and the way those roles are apportioned within the text, I shall group these characterizations of women according to their actions in the context of this book, as presented by the implied narrator: whether their deeds evoke the reader's evaluation as *positive* or *negative* and whether these deeds are *active* or *passive*. This narrowed view disregards many significant details in the individual stories, details that, however, are extraneous to the study at hand. The parameters that are used, derived from the context of the narratives, are not predetermined; indeed, they are not necessarily applicable to other biblical books.[2] They do, however, generate an overall pattern in the perception of females and their roles in the Book of Judges, summarized in table 1. This *structural* use of images of women to convey thematic and ethical motifs as well as the characters in the individual stories is subtle and sophisticated

The first female encountered in the book—Achsah, daughter of Caleb (1:12-15)—serves as a role model of propriety for later portrayals of women. For all the brevity of the episode, Achsah is not merely a two-dimensional figure: she is an individual, named and capable of initiating and completing actions. It is she who persuades her husband to ask for land, and she asks for the wells herself. The patriarchal ideal of womanhood she personifies is characterized by (1) her resourcefulness, "provoking" her husband and then petitioning her father; (2) her sexuality, as mandated within marriage and toward generation; (3) her respect toward an authoritative male figure, her father, "dropping down" before him when she makes a request of him; and (4) her acting through men rather than independently.

In contrast, Deborah's narrative describes not a young woman and bride but a mature woman, a wife (4:4) and mother (5:7) and, significantly, a woman who is prophetess and "judge" in Israel. Despite these differences, Deborah, like Achsah, is a channel for male decisions and directives: as Achsah seeks the counsel and authority of father and husband, Deborah receives the prophecies of the Lord. As the Lord's agent and deliverer, she catalyzes others to acts of deliverance. Through the authority of divine spirit, she judges the Israelites and calls males to her; but she needs Barak, a male, to fulfill her prophecies. She accompanies Barak to the battlefield but not to battle; she "draws" the fighting forces of men together (4:6-7) so that the Lord can act through them (4:15). Deborah extends the ideal of womanhood in that she may direct man to carry out the will of the Lord (presumably male), but in this text she cannot, as a female, do it herself. Achsah and Deborah, young bride and mature woman, portray the female in a positive light as both active (resourceful) and passive (accepting male authority) at two significant stages of life; together, they fulfill the criteria for such a character in this book.

This initial, positive image of woman is recalled toward the end of the cycle of judges, and once again provides a contrast: a virgin girl and a mature woman. The girl is Jephthah's daughter. Jephthah, the fatherless son of an Israelite prostitute, demonstrates almost every desirable quality for a judge, lacking only that one element that must be transmitted from one generation to another in order that the covenant be renewed and the past made present. That element is the instruction passed on from father to son, and Jephthah has no father. A condemnation of irresponsible promiscuity is implicit in Jephthah's lack of knowledge of his people's tradition. Ignorant of Israel's past, Jephthah cannot remember it, cannot participate in it, cannot renew it. When Jephthah makes a vow to observe his victory with a burnt offering, and that offering turns out to be his daughter, neither the father nor the daughter knows the Israelite tradition sufficiently to recall the story of Abraham and Isaac, which refutes human sacrifice; to seek counsel of a priest; or to offer an animal substitute.

The daughter, whose dignity mocks her lack of a name, accepts her fate, regretting not her father's vow but her virginity, her lack of progeny. As she took the initiative to welcome her father with dance, so does she make a request—one that will not compromise her father but will allow her to mourn her own death. Achsah's life-giving request from her father is echoed in this girl's request from her father for a postponement of death.

The mature counterpart to Jephthah's daughter is Manoah's wife, the mother-to-be of Samson. Like Deborah, this woman receives messages from divine messengers; but the males around her are less effective than Barak. She tells her husband, "A man of the Lord came unto me" (13:6), but he remains skeptical until the ascension of the messenger in the fire. Her actions reveal that she accepts the Israelite tradition and that she knows better than to ask the name of the divine or his messenger. In contrast, her husband, Manoah, asks, "What is your name, so that when your words came true, we may honor you?" (13:17). His question initially seems either ignorant or skeptical or both. That it is not ignorant is revealed shortly when Manoah fears death after the messenger has disappeared in the flame of the altar. Manoah knows to fear death if he has seen the face of the Lord; therefore, he undoubtedly knows not to ask the name of the Lord: both bits of information come from the same source (Exod 3:13-14). In contrast to Manoah's skepticism, his sensible wife counters his fear, saying, "If the Lord had meant to kill us, he would not have accepted a burnt offering . . . or announced to us such things as these" (13:23).

The most passive aspect of this woman's narrative is her conception. We may safely assume that the woman is a worthy recipient of divine grace or human sexuality, but there is no indication that she has even prayed for conception. Her condition was recognized and a messenger sent, as deemed necessary. She justifies the unsolicited attention by her responses: belief in the divinity of the visitor and observation of the Nazirite restrictions (see Numbers 6).

In addition to both narratives' recalling the primary female paradigms (Achsah and Deborah), Jephthah's daughter and Manoah's wife offer another interesting parallel. The sacrifice of Jephthah's daughter makes ironic allusion to the binding of Isaac, the Genesis 22 narrative in which human sacrifice is repudiated. Similarly, the annunciation to Manoah's wife recalls another Genesis passage— that of Sarah and the birth that followed: the birth of Isaac, one of the patriarchs and the father of Jacob-Israel (Genesis 18, 21). The similarity between the annunciations and impregnations of Sarah and the wife of Manoah seems to foretell another great patriarchal figure in the established tradition, a later judge worthy of his calling. Only as Samson fails to live up to these expectations is the allusion to Sarah's theophany recognized as an ironic parody. Both of these narratives make allusion to narratives in Genesis—one of death, one of birth—for ironic effects. And both women are nameless.

These four women complete the quota of women who are regarded positively in Judges, and all four are resourceful, undertaking actions but deferring to the authority of males. The women are differentiated, however, in several ways. The women have distinctly different ages: two are youthful, virgin (Jephthah's daughter) or bride (Achsah); and two are mature, wife and mother (Deborah, Manoah's wife). Moreover, individuals in the paradigm group, Achsah-Deborah, are not fully realized by their echoes in Jephthah's daughter and Manoah's wife, who, though presented positively, fail to live up to the models. The paradigm characters are named, while their successors are identified not as individuals but in terms of their closest male kin: Jephthah's daughter, Manoah's wife. All four women are characterized in terms of their sexuality: married and actively seeking reproduction (Achsah), virginal and mourning her premature death in terms of missed reproduction (Jephthah's daughter), married woman and mother (Deborah), and married woman soon to become a mother (Manoah's wife). None of these women directs her sexuality toward men outside the marriage, and none pursues sexuality as a goal in itself. Sexual pleasure for women is disregarded; the focus is on reproduction. Thus the positively presented women fall into two categories of approval, with the women "ideal" and "diminished," named and unnamed; and each category consisting of a young woman and a mature one.

We can use these women as character foils for the women who are negatively presented. Within the inclusive group of negatively presented women are three subgroups, differentiated by behavior, and each subgroup is also represented by women in youth and in maturity.

One such subset of two women is, like the positively regarded females, both actively resourceful and deferent to masculine authority. Delilah (ch. 16)—the most famous woman of this book—has become a synonym for mature, seductive woman. Although Delilah is *not* specifically identified as a prostitute, she is obviously a woman available outside the bonds of marriage, overtly using her sexual attraction to entice Samson's secret of strength from him. Inverting the paradigm male-female relationship, where the woman acts through the man, the Philistine lords act through Delilah, who accepts male authority to accomplish what the men cannot. Delilah's resourcefulness is shown in her persistent maneuvering of Samson. That she betrays for a price the man who loves her depicts Delilah as lacking ethics and morality,[3] an ironic opposite of Achsah, the bride.

The youthful counterpart to Delilah is the Levite's concubine, called "girl" until she has been raped (ch. 19). The reliable narrator says that the concubine was "unfaithful, like a harlot," to her husband, and she takes the initiative in leaving her husband to return to her parental home, assuming the male prerogative of repudiation of a partner. Whether her unfaithfulness was sexual or merely in leaving her husband, the woman has been independently active. As an indirect consequence of her action, the Levite puts his concubine out to the Gibeahites who seek *him* for sexual purposes. The end effect of her initial independent activity is her being *given* by her husband to be the *victim* of multiple rape, actions in which she is reduced to utter passivity.

The clearest distinction between the positively and negatively presented women whose actions are otherwise similar (both active and passive) is that the former are virginal or married, while the latter are involved in sexual relationships outside marriage. Since this distinction does not hold true for other negatively drawn women whose actions are entirely active or entirely passive, we may surmise that, if all else remains constant, attitudes toward sexuality may determine whether a woman is positively or negatively presented.

Among the women depicted in a negative light, two are exclusively independent, showing no deference to masculine authority whatsoever; and once again womanhood may be classified as younger and older. The younger woman is Jael, wife of Heber.[4] Jael's behavior suggests she uses her sexuality to gain her wishes, but from a man not her husband. Coming out of her tent to meet Sisera, Jael invites Sisera to "turn aside to me," to enter her tent. Furthermore, she breaks the code of host in the observance of hospitality to a guest. Jael initially seems to observe the code: she considerately covers her weary guest and brings him a choicer drink than the water he requests. In the narrative passage it is milk that she offers, but in the older poetic version (5:25) it is *hem'ah,* curd, delicious but soporific. Offering such a drink appears to be appropriate to a proper host but has elements of treachery. Indeed, she has assured him, "have no fear," but murders him as soon as possible. True, Jael gains advantage for Israel by transgressing social and ethical codes, by acting in forbidden ways: she is seductive outside her marriage, and she takes matters into her own hands, acting without the intermediary of a male figure. Jael acts, but the Lord is silent. If we are not to believe that ends define means, or that the Book of Judges has no interest in ethical behavior, we must respond to Jael negatively.

In both the Delilah and Jael narratives, which describe a male's "turning aside" to feminine enticements, the effect is disastrous for the man; but only in the Samson narrative is it immediately disastrous for Israel.[5] Men may follow women in other respects when the women, like Deborah, lead the people in the ways of the Lord; in a world of inverted values, a woman, like Manoah's wife, may lead a man to tradition. Delilah, on the other hand, actualizes the negative implications suggested in Jael's seductive actions.

Micah's mother (ch. 17), the matron counterpart to Jael's independence, does not act seductively—perhaps because she is (considered) too old. But Micah's mother introduces another problem, one that is no less profound. Although she is involved in only six verses, the consequences of her actions shape the rest of the narrative, the text suggesting that Micah has learned his ways from his mother. And her ways are not those of a male-mandated female. When she discovers her silver missing, she invokes a strong oath, a covenantal oath, *'ālah,* without benefit of a priest and for mundane rather than ethical purposes. A few verses later, the woman compounds the oath in that she blesses the confessed thief. Micah's mother seems a self-sufficient woman who acts on her own, but the text makes the reader aware that her independent actions are ill-advised, indeed, negatively regarded.

The last of this gallery of dramatized female characters are two nameless, entirely passive women who do just what they are told; and, true to the pattern, one is youthful and the other mature.

The Timnite woman (ch. 14), Samson's almost-bride, is a passive version of Delilah: she foreshadows Delilah when she betrays her husband to her people—not willfully, for a price, as Delilah does, but under threat of destruction by fire. Although both the Timnite woman and Delilah cajole secrets from Samson, both under "orders" from men, the Timnite woman makes no independent decision to act. If she does not comply, the men will burn down her house and that of her father (14:15). Delilah is not forced into betrayal: of her own will, she accepts a business proposition from the Philistine lords: Samson's secrets for silver. The Timnite woman is, by contrast, coerced into complicity.

His riddle answered, Samson abandons his Timnite wife in anger; but when his desire returns, his anger cools; and "after a while" he seeks to visit his wife, obviously to "know" her sexually (ch. 15). Her father had already given her (again a passive recipient of masculine will) to the best man, taking her as hated by her husband; and Samson seeks revenge, which ironically leads to the bride and her family being destroyed by fire—exactly that which the

Table 1: Characterization in the Book of Judges

Independent/Active	Dependent/Passive	Youthful	Mature
Dramatized Women			
Positive Presentation			
X			Deborah
	X		Manoah's wife
X		Achsah	
	X	Jephthah's daughter	
X		Woman of Thebes	
Negative Presentation			
X			Delilah
X			Micah's mother
	X		Whore of Gaza
X		Levite's concubine	
X		Jael	
	X	Timnite woman	
Undramatized Women			
	X	Daughters of Jabesh-Gilead	Gilead's wives/concubines
	X	Daughters of Shiloh	Harlot mother of Jephthah

Table 1: Characterization in the Book of Judges

Timnite woman sought to avoid by following the advice of her countrymen and betraying her husband.

The mature woman who serves to complete this pair of nameless, passive women is a female who is presented solely as a sexual object: the whore of Gaza (16:1-3). Entirely passive, she manages to keep Samson entertained only until midnight, which allows him enough time to uproot the city gates and carry them to Hebron. Although the Timnite woman is a young bride and the whore of Gaza an experienced prostitute, both passive women are characterized as sexual objects.

This almost schematic balance of characterizations is rendered ambiguous by one character who resists classification, refusing to conform. The woman of Thebez is scarcely dramatized (but neither is Samson's whore of Gaza). Dropping a millstone on Abimelech's head (9:53-54), this woman acts without divine or earthly male advice; yet her actions can only bring cheers from the reader. Furthermore, there is no record that she consulted a male before taking action. One may well question that the woman who acts solely on her own initiative in this story generates approval, contradictory to the other narratives. This is, however, consistent with the world in which this woman operates: the world of the Deborah-Jael narrative is consistent with YHWH; that of the Abimelech narrative is antagonistic. Actions and their values are inverted in the world of Abimelech, and it may be that in a world where man has transposed values, woman may do what is normally wrong and achieve good. As an ironic parody, the woman of Thebez may be regarded as positive in her inverted world but negative in the normative world.

Finally, some women are mentioned but not dramatized. These women all serve passive functions and, like the paired groups above, are youthful and mature. The concubine and multiple wives of Gideon and the harlot mother of Jephthah are nameless women who have served reproductive or sexual roles in the narrative sequence but are not further differentiated. Gideon's foreign concubine gives birth to Abimelech, who destroys all but one of the legitimate sons of Gideon's wives. Jephthah's harlot mother cannot transmit the tradition that is passed from father to son, which leads to the termination of his line. In contrast with these sexually "knowing" women, the virgin daughters of Jabesh-gilead and

Shiloh who are kidnapped in ch. 21 are victims rendered as objects for reproduction, implicitly disparaged as objects for sexuality. Even in these undramatized references, role values are strongly insinuated; and sexual roles play a significant part in determining positive or negative appraisal. The narratives repeatedly and consistently disdain extramarital sexuality,[6] even if it serves the all-important demand for generation and multiplication of the people. The contrast of the virgins kidnapped for marriage at the end of the book with Achsah, a reward in marriage at the opening, suggests that marriage is not merely a device to whitewash all behavior. It involves respect and esteem of an active partner within the framework of the tradition.

This is an extraordinary array of characters, especially when we find a pattern: paired girl and mature woman in each mode of behavior. However, the design is not as significant as the knowledge it makes overt: in a range of narrative functions, females are presented—implicitly judged—according to masculine-determined concepts of acceptable and nonacceptable roles for women, and female sexuality is a significant constraint.

The Book of Judges:
Paradigm and Deviation in Images of Women

This structural pattern of women may be explored in another way: according to the character and role of the individual woman. As a book structured around paradigm and repeated ironic deviation in masculine behavior, Judges is consistent in presenting a brief but symbolically rich depiction of a model woman in its opening chapter (1:12-15) and ironic reversals of that paradigm in the final two dramatizations of women (16:4-23; 17:1-6).[7] This juxtaposition of extremes illuminates the structure of the book as well as the implications of the proffered paradigm for women.[8]

In a few terse lines (1:12-15), the Book of Judges offers an image of a model woman in a model male-female relationship. That the image is a paradigm is verified by the structure of the book: this image of woman is subsequently contrasted with other images of woman, all deficient in one or more ways; and the relationship is subsequently contrasted with more-than-deficient relationships between men and women.

Admittedly, this initial presentation does not offer an encompassing feminine ideal. It is an exemplar, limited by brevity and context. Nevertheless, it offers the reader an opportunity to glean what this text suggests as the qualities and behavior valued in a woman.

The entire story of Achsah, her father Caleb and her bridegroom Othniel takes place in only four verses: Judg. 1:12-15. The first mention of Achsah occurs when Caleb offers her as wife to the man who attacks *Kiriath-sepher* and takes it (1:12). Caleb seems to place great value on his daughter, awarding her to a warrior as a prize for the man's service to his people. For modern readers, there may even be an aura of romance around the lure of a commander's daughter being given in marriage as a stimulus for bravery in righteous battle. The Hebrew Bible, however, does not project such a romantic view. The future husband sought is not a strong man (*'îš gādôl*), or even a man (*'îš*). He is referred to by a subordinating word translated here as "who" (*'ašer*): "who strikes and captures" the city. The "hero" is merely the man who does the job.

Achsah is proffered as reward—an object of value as extraordinary compensation (tribute) for an extraordinary job well done. As object, Achsah is not consulted for approval of her husband. He could be a man old enough to be her father, a man ripe in battle experience, or even a youngster with unusual skill and luck, a David against a Goliath city. Achsah, a passive agent of her father's wishes, is given to the man who accomplishes the feat. The first verse, then, presents the modern reader with distinct but not contradictory impressions: woman is at once valued and a passive object in the patriarchal system. In this portrayal, males desire and value woman as an object of exchange and ultimate control.

Ultimate control but not total control. As wife of Othniel, Achsah initiates some actions on her own, and her initial action involves her husband. Achsah loses no time: she begins "as she came" or "in her coming" (Hebrew root: *bw'*), a word-phrase that refers both to her coming to her bridegroom and to sexual intercourse. The former connotation informs the reader that Achsah goes to her husband's family in the preferred patrilocal marriage. This form of marriage also enables the husband's control of his wife since she is in his territory, among his relatives. That the woman is not without protection is alluded to in the identification of Othniel as a nephew of Caleb—the son of a younger brother, Kenaz. Such marriages between cousins guarantee that the bride is not very far from her own family's quarters and is represented in case of marital difficulties. Achsah, then, has nothing to fear in going to her husband's family since her own family is not distant geographically. She is protected in serious circumstances, but the day-to-day living is in her husband's environment, where he can exercise most control with least effort. And "as she came"—that is, immediately—she presents a task to her husband.

A second implication of the phrase "as she came" suggests that Achsah waited until the marriage was consummated to express her wishes; more pointedly, she waited until after sexual intercourse to make her wishes known. This passage implies that women may, are even expected to, make requests when the man is pleasantly weak with sexual satisfaction. The woman, however, is not weak: Achsah clearly uses the moment to her advantage. She is not depicted as a hesitant, timid little bride in awe of her warrior husband; she is a resourceful and determined woman who knows what she wants and how to realize her objectives in her culture. For Achsah does not make a request of her husband; she "incites" (Hebrew root: *syt*), almost harries him to do her bidding: make a request of her father.[9] German translations of this verb—*verlocken,* to entice, tempt; *verführen,* to tempt, to seduce, to encourage someone to do something—reinforce the sexual component of "as she came."[10]

In some translations, Achsah's actions have been masked one way or another; in almost all they have been softened. For instance, the Septuagint and Vulgate translations "correct" the identity of the instigator: "and she came and *he* persuaded *her* to ask," justified so that "the request does not come from Achsah"[11] or "to preserve the image of the first savior judge."[12] Other translations soften the verb from "incite" to gentler verbs, like "persuade."[13] We note that Achsah does not "persuade"; she "incites" her husband, possibly sexually, in order to realize her wishes.

Within marriage, the text suggests, the wife's ability to initiate actions, even to bring the husband to action, is emphasized. Just as Judges depicts women as objects of man's control, it extols women who take initiative within the constraints of patriarchal mores.[14]

Control is more gratifying when the object is intelligent and stimulating and, the text suggests, a man may be made malleable. Othniel understandably complies with his wife's strongly conveyed, sexually linked wishes. Here the text suggests that wives can influence their all-powerful husbands by using their sexuality—by being gratifying objects of sexual desire. Women, then, are potentially objects of masculine pawn before marriage and are compliant, if not stimulating, objects of sexuality after marriage, that is, if they want to have their wishes realized.[15]

In this instance, Achsah's forcefully expressed wish is that her husband ask her father for a piece of land, a field. Achsah's wish for a field implies that she desires to plant seed, to generate; her wish, as will be seen, can be taken to symbolize human as well as plant procreation. Thus the text suggests that the concerns of a paradigm woman are with generation and regeneration.

Othniel's actual request to Caleb is subsumed and the same verse continues with Achsah's second action, her own request from her father. This central verse of the mininarrative is the most terse, combining two distinct actions through the linkage of one actor and a simple *waw* conversive. Achsah's actions are the key of the narrative, and they are relative to her husband and her father in the two sections of the verse. The sequence of husband-father also suggests that the woman's close relationship with her father continues after marriage.[16]

As the action of the first part of 1:14 is governed by two significant verbs, *bw'* and *syt,* the second half of the verse also presents a key verb, but this verb is more problematic. Sexual innuendoes are not present in *tiṣnaḥ,* the verb of the father-daughter relationship; but the meaning of this verb is more elusive.[17] In extraordinarily elliptical language, Achsah approaches her father on an ass, descends from the ass, and lowers herself before her father. The Hebrew is so concentrated that it almost sounds like Achsah falls off her donkey before her father. That she gets down from her donkey is unimportant; what matters is that she shows her father utmost respect, "dropping down" before him. The approach and the descent are implicit, and *tiṣnaḥ* may be understood as Achsah's prostrating herself before her father. Caleb's response, literally "What for you?" completes the verse. Like any father through the ages, Caleb is not used to his daughter's greeting him in this fashion and

asks, essentially, "What is the matter with you?" Achsah knows the
gender rules of her culture, and Caleb seems to recognize that
obeisance from a woman involves a wish. Achsah seduces her husband and adduces her father, leading the latter to her desires
through supplication and logic.

Her desire in this instance is water, the second factor in generation. Her objective in both her requests is to plant seed, to become a
fruitful mother. Motherhood is a biological role; it is also the sole
social role demonstrated in two significant, if concise, exchanges.

The terse, highly symbolic language of this key verse gives way to
fuller narration as Achsah speaks. She does not, however, immediately ask for water; she asks for a *b^erakah*, a blessing. In this form,
the noun can refer either to an ascription of praise to (or from)
God, or to a gift, a present. When Achsah asks for a *b^erakah*, she at
once asks for a present from her father and symbolically elevates
him to a Godlike position. Her request is for something that only
God can give, since the land is held to belong to God. Caleb "gives"
her water, having "given" her husband land; in so doing, he gives her
a blessing: giving what only God can give, he completes the conditions for fertility.

Symbolically, Achsah represents all Israel as a bride to God, and
her obeisance to her father represents man's obeisance to God. The
hierarchy of God-man-woman is explicit. Achsah, as low "man" on
this totem pole, is obeisant to and flatters her father—in the highest
degree—in order to gain her desires. God wants man's obeisance;
man wants woman's. But just as man can plead, pray, talk, even
"haggle" with God (Gen 18:22-23), woman can use any socially acceptable device that works to realize her wishes from man.

Achsah's approach to her father is to humble herself, to flatter
him, and to make requests that are befitting a woman, requests that
further generation; and her delivery is so effective that her father
gives not one but two sources of water, the "upper springs" and the
"lower springs." One may recognize a sexual image in the male's giving fluid—exuberantly, two springs—to the female but dismiss it
because of the father-daughter relationship. The father's participat-
ing in the sexual image, however, represents him as still potent and
in a position to enhance his daughter's reproductive role, albeit indirectly. Caleb is presented in a position of authority and abun-

dance. Virility thus seems to imply power in the wider sense of social power. This sexual-social power is clearly under man's ultimate
control in this narrative: Achsah must act through men (her husband) or request from men (her father). As depicted in this narrative, she is clever and resourceful, initiating social actions on the
part of males within the constraints of the patriarchal system and
her social role in that system.

This mininarrative portrays a woman who can gain her wishes—
wishes established as permissible by the community—through her
appeals to the men who have authority over her: her husband and
her father. Masterfully created, the text demonstrates both the constraints of women's roles and the range of power women are free to
exercise within those limitations. Achsah, as paradigm woman,
knows how to use her influence to realize her wishes, and she is
amply rewarded: she and her husband receive land to plant seed,
and she is given not one well but two. She constitutes an ideal
woman in the patriarchal system. She also reminds her father and
husband—paradigm men—of more basic truths than the wars the
men of Israel are engaged in: earth, water, regeneration.

The transition from the cyclical narratives of Judges to the resolution of the book is linked by two sequential narratives that introduce the motif of silver, and in both instances a woman and silver
are associated with values improper for the Israelite community.
The contrasts in the two situations invite a closer examination of
the texts to determine what the images of contamination of the
ideal have to say about woman and her function in society.

The first narrative (Judges 16) concerns Delilah, infamous to
modern readers as the woman who seduced the love-stricken Samson to reveal the secret of his strength for a goodly sum of silver:
eleven hundred pieces from each of the Philistine rulers who proposed the scheme.

Despite her reputation, the Delilah of the text is more complex
and more interesting as a character than a mere one-dimensional
seductress. She is not identified by the name of her hometown, but
only by a region, the *naḥal śōrēq*. This is particularly noteworthy in
a sequence that includes far more proper names of settlements than
any other narrative in the book: Zorah, Eshtaol, Timnat, Ashkelon,
Lehi, Hebron, and Gaza. The only other places left unspecified are

the "Camp of Dan," which apparently was not a permanent settlement with a proper name, and the "Rock of Etam," a geological feature. Indeed, Delilah is associated with a rather large territory: the *naḥal śōrēq,* now called *Wadi es-Sarar,* is one of many wadis or flood beds that carry water down from the higher regions, in this case from the hills of Judah. The *naḥal śōrēq* describes a geographic area that cuts through the harsh Judean hills, on the one hand, to the fertile coastal range, on the other.

The first term in Delilah's area of identification, *naḥal,* refers to the wadi. With the rains, these become virtual torrents; and the word "torrent" is a more appropriate translation than "valley," which suggests a stable landscape with a "creek," a tranquil water route. The second term, *śōrēq,* alludes to a choice of wine grape and associates Delilah with the pleasant but dangerous loss of control identified with wine. Delilah is mingled with uncontrolled "torrents" and control-eroding wine, both strongly suggestive of overwhelming passions. Furthermore, Delilah is not identified through a male kinsman. She is an unattached woman, and such women are often depicted as seductively leading potentially good men astray.

The connotations of Delilah's dwelling place—literally a "torrent bed," a place where water (a symbol of fertility) now and then courses—further qualify the character of this woman, without roots in history or land, associated with passion. The text does not specify that she has a price for her companionship as well as for her betrayal, and since the whore of Gaza is specifically identified as such, we must seek further significance in Delilah's role.

As a Philistine,[18] Delilah's genealogy is inconsequential for an Israelite narrative. That neither her father (nor her husband, if any) nor her city is cited, however, makes her virtually rootless in time (no genealogical line) and place (no place of origin). This is suggestive in a literature that emphasizes the continuity of generations and distinguishes the "sons of Israel" from the rootless "nations." Delilah is presented as an unusually independent woman who engages in direct commercial enterprises with men and uses her sexuality to tangible advantage.[19]

Delilah's activities split the "prostitute"-male relationship into two: one man "loves" her, another (actually "others") pay her. She "sells herself" but clouds the issue with a bifurcated transaction,

[handwritten margin note: lack of geneology, independent, advantageous, "other" = evil]

which makes Delilah more interesting than the simple prostitute of Gaza. In fact, Delilah's lack of clarity about her relations damns her as the worst of the three "lovers" in Samson's narrative: his wife betrays Samson out of fear, the whore of Gaza neither betrays nor assists the man who is merely her "client," and Delilah, the woman he loves, betrays him for the lowest of purposes: a price. To the Israelite reader, Delilah is depicted as worse than a prostitute, a claim supported by her appearance as the female climax in Judges' cyclical sequence of flawed characters.

Prostitute or not, the methods Delilah uses are acceptable, perhaps traditional, even if she uses them not to stimulate the processes of natural fertility (as in cultic "prostitution") but to aid her people more directly (eliminating an outside threat). Delilah may not be associated with prostitution at all; she may simply be using Samson's love for her to aid her people. The ambiguities of the text must be held in tandem by the reader. However, this very ambiguity stresses that the Israelite male cannot comprehend foreign women—their words, their values, their allegiances. Being in love compounds the difficulty.

tools for division + promoting "otherness"

Ritual "prostitution" was a form of sympathetic magic, initiating and stimulating fertility by means of intercourse with worshippers. Delilah and the Philistines seek the magic secret of "in what [lies] his great strength" (16:5). Delilah may be using her culture's "magic" to expose what the Philistines understand as the "magic" of Samson's strength. Delilah is offered 1,100 pieces of silver from each of the Philistine leaders who devise the scheme, and when she sends for the Philistines, they bring the silver payment with them. The text implies that women who offer their services for payment are automatically derogated in the Israelite culture. Delilah is probably not paid for her sexual services, since she is not described as a prostitute; she is paid for providing information about Samson's strength. It is clear that the only way the men can imagine her gleaning that information is through emotional and sexual weakening of the man's resolutions. It is, after all, the men who direct Delilah in how to learn the secret of Samson's strength.

The reader is invited to scorn Delilah because she uses Samson's love to get what she wants from him. This may or may not be prescribed for women in the Philistine culture, but it does seem to be a role given to women in Israelite society: they are to manipulate men with sexual favors within marriage or by obeisant requests otherwise, as Achsah does. In fact, Delilah never says she loves Samson, which discloses an integrity of a sort: she does not compromise her emotions; she uses his.

Finally, Delilah's approach to Samson is nothing if not direct. She may believe that love not only makes lovers blind but also stupid, for Samson certainly does not profit either from his wife's cajoling or Delilah's repeated attempts to gain the secret of his strength. She puts pressure on him over many days until his spirit is worn out—"to death"—but the text never suggests she is devious. She repeatedly says exactly what she wants:

> Now tell me in what your great strength lies and with what you may be bound in order to afflict you. (16:6)

> Behold, you have ridiculed me and told me lies; now please tell me with what you may be bound. (16:10)

> Until now you have ridiculed me and have told me lies; tell me with what you may be bound. (16:13)

> How can you say, I love you, when your heart is not with me. You have ridiculed me these three times but you have not told me in what your great strength lies. (16:15)

Delilah is openly manipulating Samson according to the best Israelite standards.

The sequence of speeches also conceals, in the progression of "key terms," a more subtle expression of Delilah's objectives: in the sequence of speeches, one element is retained in each new formulation.[20]

Philistines	16:5	strength	*bind*	maltreatment
First speech	16:6	strength	*binding*	maltreatment
Second speech	16:10	*ridicule*	lies	*binding*
Third speech	16:13	*ridicule*	lies	*binding*
Fourth speech	16:15	love	*ridicule*	strength

In this analysis, verses are paired off by repetition of the three key elements, and one element from each pair of lines shifts one position in the subsequent formulation. "Bind/binding" shifts from second to third element, and "ridicule" shifts from first to second. The last element, "strength," frames a closure with the first. When the key elements are grouped according to recurrence, a pattern emerges:

binding	4	
strength	3	ridicule
lies	2	maltreatment
	1	love

The most repeated element in the Philistine verbal attack is "binding"; that which the Philistine leaders primarily desire is repeated by their accomplice to a total of four times. "Strength" and "ridicule," each iterated three times (twice as a first element in a verse), contrasts Samson's divine resource and Delilah's very *human* perception of his evasiveness—both important to Delilah. Likewise, "lies" and "maltreatment" contrast the efforts of Samson and Delilah (Israel/Philistine) on a somewhat more earthly and less intense level, twice each. The least important element on Delilah's tongue, mentioned only once, is that which makes Samson "weak" to her "love." Knowing that these are Philistine-Delilah's words, the reader recognizes that love is literally one of the last things that occurs to her. The terms "binding" and "love" are opposed from Delilah's viewpoint but one and the same from Samson's, for love binds him to Delilah. These dual viewpoints may also be extended to Israelite and Philistine perceptions of Delilah.

Delilah's not loving Samson implies that, in the view of this narrator, woman can resist man. Samson is not loved by the woman he loves; in fact, she uses his desires to achieve her goals. The text reveals Samson as incapable of hearing anything but his own love, his own desires. The reader is encouraged both to pity the poor, lovelorn Samson and to mock the fool that allows himself to become subject to woman. Delilah, the spurning woman, seems evil incarnate; for Samson offers Delilah love, and she uses his love to bring about his downfall at the hands of his enemies. Delilah strikes Samson at the one spot where he has no strength.

On the other hand, Delilah is true to her own culture. The reader may not appreciate that the tables are being turned against the Israelites, but Delilah cannot be faulted for serving her people. That an exchange of money is involved suggests a variant on "prostitution," anathema to the Israelites. This is reinforced in the text, which specifies that "the lords of the Philistines *came up to her*" (16:5). Delilah's residence is located higher than the coastal cities of the Philistines; the "high places" are also associated with cultic copulation. However, as mentioned above, "prostitution" in the service of the culture was probably a modus vivendi among the Philistines;[21] and Delilah, as a Philistine, cannot be judged by Israelite standards. Delilah is simultaneously protecting her people and is reviled by the reader in sympathy with the Israelites. Furthermore, the Philistine lords' demanding her betrayal of her lover does not imply its morality for that culture; political acts are not famous for their ethics. Delilah presents a complex picture of a resourceful woman, possibly a heroine to her own people, who perpetrates an age-old and repugnant ruse: using a man's love to bring him down. The narrator seems to expect women to use men's weaknesses; nevertheless, the text faults women that do not use this power the way men want them to.

A somewhat different situation is encountered in the next narrative (17:1-5). Micah's mother—otherwise unnamed—is addressed by her son, who tells her he took the 1,100 pieces of silver that she is missing. The sum of 1,100 pieces of silver is a tangible link to the Delilah narrative, and the reader is alerted to the comparisons and contrasts the narratives offer.

Whatever the reader's response to Delilah's actions, the mother-of-Micah narrative strongly intensifies the negative implications. The high price of betrayal, perhaps warranted by personal values and/or danger from Delilah's perspective, remains the same—1,100 pieces of silver; but bribe money becomes stolen money, for in the Micah narrative, the silver is unquestionably stolen, not exchanged between consenting parties. Worse, Micah betrays the trust of blood-tie, of mother-son kinship. The former exchange was between Philistines, not Israelites, on a "business basis": a set fee for a specific service. There is no call for Micah, as there is for Delilah, to protect his people from a threatening force; and there is no financial need. The son, male and younger, vandalizes his mother, female and elder, thus turning upside down the covenantal and cultural structure of respect and protection. Delilah, the gauge of evil—foreigner, seductress, betrayer—is surpassed by Micah and his mother, Israelite betrayers of Israelite values without reason.

Micah initiates the narrative conflict, but let us concentrate on his mother. She has, Micah tells us, "uttered a curse." The noun used, *'ālah,* means "to invoke God": the primary meaning of *'ālah* is "oath, especially a covenant made by an oath."[22] The import here rests not with the contents of the oath but that the woman took it upon herself to make an oath *with this word.*[23]

The use of *'ālah* is selective and infrequent in the preceding books of the Hebrew Bible. Abraham had caused his servant to swear, using *šb'*, to bring back a bride for Isaac only from Abraham's family; but in his recounting of the event the servant elevated the occasion to a covenantal oath, *'ālah* (Gen. 24:41). The term is used by Abimelech in his recognition of YHWH when he asks Isaac for a covenant of peace (Gen. 26:29). Finally, at the threshold of the promised land, Moses calls the entire people to him that they may enter into the covenant and the oath with YHWH, to establish them on that day as YHWH's people (Deut. 29:12, 14). Clearly the word is used with special reverence. Yet this word is used by Micah's mother to invoke a covenant with YHWH without benefit of a priest, and for mundane rather than ethical purposes: to regain her silver.

A few verses later, the woman blesses the thief, her son, by YHWH, because he has returned what he stole. Micah's mother apparently uses YHWH's name much as Micah will seek to use YHWH, for convenience: she assumes the right to make oaths and invoke blessings, and to do these things on behalf of a worldly tangible. Her consecration of the silver further maligns her ties to the Israelite tradition, for she withholds the far greater sum (900 pieces of silver); and the 200 she does expend are used to make an image, expressly forbidden by YHWH. Micah has learned his mother's values and will shortly involve the third generation, his son, in a practice of what is, in fact, anticovenantal but believed to be dedicated to YHWH. The deterioration from the ethical covenant that once marked YHWH's people is shown being passed from generation to generation and becoming entrenched and established. With the economy typical of biblical style and with narrative objectivity that does not judge the events described—that is left to the reader—the first three verses relate the desecration of as many commandments.[24] Micah's mother is directly responsible for the first violation, and, the text implies, indirectly responsible for her son's anticovenantal behavior.

When we compare Delilah and Micah's mother, Delilah profits enormously. But the net effect is more ominous: both images of women defame the women and provide at least an escape hatch for the less-than-desirable behavior of the men. Samson is in love with Delilah and therefore susceptible to the wiles of women; Micah is the product of his mother's upbringing and cannot know any better. The women, whether they act as agents of men (Delilah) or on their own (Micah's mother), do wrong, and without any apparent justification in the view of Israelites; in the case of Micah's mother, the wrongs are compounded. Delilah's wrong doing is based on her taking directions from the wrong men, in the view of the Israelites; otherwise men lead women to doing right, as with Achsah, Caleb and Othniel. The net effect is that this text depicts women as acceptable only when they further man's concepts of himself. Women acting on their own are shown to act wrongly and to pass their misjudgments on to further generations, thus undermining the social structure.[25]

These two narratives allow women little room to contribute to society or to create satisfying lives for themselves. But women can glean positive directions by reading these same texts closely. Delilah's narrative suggests that women (like men) may have difficulty distinguishing ethical from cultural values when they are closely intermeshed. That she sells her services—possibly to Samson, clearly to the Philistine lords—is socially approved in her culture. But Micah's mother distorts Israelite tradition out of lack of knowledge, and no husband is present to offer the necessary balance that comes with knowledge. This narrative makes explicit what develops when women are kept uninstructed: they pass on their ignorance. Delilah understands her culture and is true to it; Micah's mother fails on both counts even though she considers herself a good, devoted follower of YHWH.

We note that there is no mention of a father in the narrative of Micah and his mother. Micah, as son, must learn from his father; but when the father is absent from the family for whatever reason, it may fall to the mother to raise her son, to teach him the ways of his religion and his culture.[26] The texts, however, offer no evidence of education for females of the culture. The distortion associated with Micah's mother may be a result of inadequate education for females; and since Micah seems to lack a father, he also lacks the education his father would provide. Boys are circumcised shortly after birth, a ritual that literally marks their involvement, to be emotionally and intellectually developed by their fathers as they develop. Girls, however, are neither symbolically nor literally educated into the system of religious or ethical knowledge.

Yet this is contradictory to the precepts set forth by Moses in Deuteronomy, one of the books of prescriptive laws:

And Moses summoned *all* Israel, and said to them, "Hear, O Israel, the statutes and the ordinances which I speak in your hearing this day, and you shall learn them and be careful to do them." (5:1, NEB)

. . . when *all Israel* comes to appear before YHWH your God at the place which he will choose, you shall read this law before *all Israel* in their hearing. (my emphasis, 31:11, NEB)

Lest "all Israel" be taken to mean only the males, the following passage is even more explicit:

Assemble the *people, men, women* and *little ones,* and the sojourner within your towns, that they may hear and learn to fear YHWH your God, and be careful to do all the words of this law. (31:12)

and that their *children,* who have not known it, may hear and learn to fear YHWH your God. (my emphasis, 31:13, NEB)

Moses recognized that men *and women* must hear and learn in order to practice and propagate the faith and the culture. The Book of Judges implies that the men who continued the tradition lacked Moses' understanding and failed to hear and learn this basic and profound precept.[27] Thus the very men who bemoan the degradation of the Israelites ensure that very condition by failing to ascertain that the girls—the future women—of the community will understand and practice the religious and cultic rituals. Delilah knows the ways of her culture; Micah's mother—and Micah—dramatize the consequences of not assuring that women be included in the knowledge as well as the experience of cultic life.

Achsah, as paradigm woman, concerns herself with generation and realizes her wishes through prescribed interaction with relational males. There is no suggestion that she is or will become culturally or economically independent. Both Delilah and Micah's mother are, by comparison, single women who act for their own interests, not for generation, and both are described in compromising situations and actions. Juxtaposition of these narrative sequences suggests that women were both feared and respected, which perhaps made it seem necessary that they be curtailed in their freedom by restrictive paradigms, and that deviation from these paradigms be associated with anticovenantal behavior.

We can recognize three roles of behavior attributed to women. Achsah is a woman who behaves in ways approved by the male society, even though men carry out the actions to realize her regenerative wishes. Delilah reverses Achsah's paradigm: she carries out the actions males desire. Furthermore, Delilah is apparently not concerned with generation. Micah's mother represents a third potential for active women: no males are involved as authority. Micah's mother attests to her concern with generation, having borne at least one son; but the family structure seems as distorted as Micah's mother's concept of YHWH.

The paradigm of Achsah as ideal in this book establishes a norm for subsequent deviations. But it also becomes evident that the patriarchal writers created a double bind: women are uneducated because men fail to observe the strictures of the Mosaic covenant, and women are then faulted for behaving in anticovenantal ways. The Book of Judges discloses a no-win situation for both men and women.

Deborah and Jael:
Audacious Female Role Models?

*D*eborah is an anomaly. She is notably distinctive in the wide range and nature of her narrative roles: she is a judge and a prophet: a woman who sits in judgment of men and speaks as an oracle of YHWH. It would seem that Deborah is truly a woman in a position of power in the world of men, but we will see that the narrative binds her with constraints on all sides.

Deborah is described as "wife of Lappidot." No other information about Deborah's husband is provided. "Lappidot" is usually translated as "torches"; this is the only time that the word occurs in the Bible: his name is a *hapax legomenon*. The very strangeness of his name may suggest a remarkable quality, perhaps that the function of Deborah's husband in this narrative is comparable to the function of many narrative women, wives: in the background, without a voice. Later Deborah is also called a mother (Judg 5:7), although it is not clear whether she is a "national" mother or an ordinary mother of children. The narrative may show a woman in an unusual position of apparent power, but does it suggest role exchange (how modern!), the possible feminization of a male? Deborah, as a female judge and prophet, is embedded in tradition as well as in literature. Not subject to erasure, does Deborah embody a reversal of literary roles as an implicit warning to men of the possible consequences of women in public life? A woman of her stature never reappears in biblical literature.

a sexist patriarchal cautionary tale

Finally, "Deborah" means "bee." It is curious that the book that celebrates an abundance of milk and honey mentions the source of that honey, the bee, only once in the singular (Isa 7:18), three times in the plural (Deut 1:44; Judg 14:18; Ps 118:12), and as the name of two women: Rebecca's nurse and Deborah the judge.[1] The four references to the bee, furthermore, are unusually negative, associating the bee of clean habits with the notoriously filthy fly or depicting bees as vanquishers and attackers of men. Only the reference to bees in Samson's exploits associates bees with honey, but even in that passage the bee is stigmatized as living and producing in decaying flesh, totally contrary to the facts of nature. Heinrich Margulies,[2] who advanced this argument, suggests that biblical redactors have taken care to eradicate or denigrate references to bees because of their association with another matriarchal figure, the Mother Earth of Aegean, especially Cretan, mythology.[3]

Even more remarkable is Deborah's public association with another man, Barak, her military leader. Interestingly, the name of Barak means "flash of lightning."[4] Thus Deborah seems to function on the social level (as wife) and on the spiritual level (as prophet), uniting both as judge; and she does so between two poles of light or fire: a "torch" and a "flash of lightning."

Deborah may be an unexpected choice for a judge and prophet, but she has already been functioning in that capacity at the opening of the narrative. She has an established "court" location under a palm named for her, "the palm of Deborah," important enough to be identified with specific directions as to location: "between Ramah and Bethel in the hill country of Ephraim" (4:4). This information establishes the tradition and suggests the longevity of Deborah's tenure as judge. Lest there be any doubt as to her position, the text spells it out quite clearly: "and the Israelites came up to her for judgment" (4:5).

Deborah assumes a very masculine role when she "sent and summoned Barak" to come to her (4:6). Though women may indeed direct male activities, I cannot think of another instance when a woman demands a man respond to her command in this tone.[5] Yet Deborah does not command Barak in her own person. She speaks as an agent of YHWH:

Has not Yahweh, God of Israel, commanded? Go and draw toward
Mount Tabor and take ten thousand men of the sons of Naphtali
and the sons of Zebulun, and I will draw to you Sisera the captain of
the army of Jabin, to meet you by the river Kishon with his chariots
and his multitude and I shall give him into your hands. (4:6)

Barak is to deploy a specific number of men from two named
tribes at a specific location. She herself will "draw out" Sisera, the
enemy general, and "give him" with his troops and chariots into
Barak's hands at another position (4:6-7). Although Deborah
speaks with authority, her words are prefaced by their divine source:
Deborah appears to be a voice—one that just happens to be female—through whom God speaks.

Note that Barak's response is constructed formally, explicitly: "If
you will go with me, I will go; but if you will not go with me, I will
not go" (4:8).

No condensation, no allusion, no subtlety here; and no chias-
mus, frequent when terms are repeated. Although the tone is decisive, the content suggests dependence, insecurity. This is a man who
knows his own limitations. The certainty of Deborah's voice is emphasized by the doubt in Barak's, who only agrees to go if Deborah
will go with him! These exaggerated role reversals draw attention to
divine power, the power behind Deborah's voice, which can make a
mere woman strong and certain, and ridicules male power, dependent and fearful even in a military figure.

In reply to Barak's doubts, Deborah's statement is poised and
serenely controlled: "I will surely go[6] with you; only your glory shall
not be *on the way which you are going*, for YHWH will sell Sisera into
the hand of a woman" (4:9, my italics).

Deborah's tone borders on disdain as she assures Sisera she will
accompany him, and she concludes with a reproof. "On the way
which you are going" is ambiguous: it could mean the literal path he
chooses to take, and it could also refer to his reluctance to respond
positively to the prophetess' call to action. The prediction Deborah
makes, that Sisera will be conquered by a woman, is primarily and
powerfully insulting. She is foretelling that the commanding military leader will be upstaged by a mere woman. The reader, naturally,
assumes that the woman who will conquer Sisera is Deborah, but

her speech will prove to be more subtle, suggestive, symbolic. For the moment, comparison of the direct speeches of Barak and Deborah gains the reader's attention. Barak follows Deborah's orders explicitly, calling together the forces of the tribes she specified, in her role as prophet, and leading them, with Deborah, to the battle site, Kadesh.

With Barak and Deborah en route, the narrative shifts to the tent of Heber the Kenite, who had been separated from his people and set up his tent at a site near the projected battlefield. Abruptly, the scene shifts again, this time to the enemy camp, where Sisera learns that Barak had left for Mount Tabor, for battle. (Although Barak's mission was dependent upon the presence of Deborah, no mention of her is made to Sisera, perhaps because the presence of a prophetess on the battlefield was probably of no significance to a non-Israelite military commander.) With this news, Sisera calls together his nine hundred iron chariots and all the people with him. All the pieces are in place and the action can begin.

Yet another delaying tactic intercedes: Deborah predicts to Barak that he shall have success in the battle: "Rise up, for this is the day in which YHWH *has given* Sisera into your hand; has not YHWH *gone* out before you?" (4:14, my italics).

There seems to be a contradiction between Deborah's earlier statement and this one: earlier she said that a *woman* would conquer Sisera and now that *Barak* will conquer Sisera. The narrative suggests that Deborah has seen, in prophecy, all that will transpire, which allows her to speak with the utmost authority of the outcome of the day's events, describing them in the past tense because she has already seen them happen.

The battle is won by YHWH, who "destroyed Sisera, and all the chariots and all the army, by the edge of the sword, before Barak" (4:15). Barak pursues the chariots and the army and destroys every last one. Sisera, however, escapes from his chariot and flees on foot. With this information, we can deduce that "Sisera" refers both to the man, the individual, and to his armies. Barak/YHWH have indeed destroyed Sisera—the armies of Sisera—but the individual is still afoot. His army destroyed, Sisera the man flees to the tent of Heber the Kenite, "for there was peace between Jabin the king of Hazor and the house of Heber the Kenite" (4:17).[7] One detail is missing. The wife of Heber the Kenite is Jael. The nationality of Jael is not provided, but her actions suggest that she may be an Israelite. The name "Jael" means "ibex," a graceful wild goat with curving horns that is native to the land. The name is suggestive.

Jael is quite as independent a woman as Deborah. She not only welcomes a man outside the family into her tent, but goes outside to meet him, to look for him, to invite him: "And Jael went out to meet Sisera, and said to him, "Turn aside, my lord, turn aside to me; do not fear; and he turned aside to her, into the tent, and she covered him with a rug [or a fly net]" (4:18).

Jael's invitation is suspect from the beginning. A woman inviting a man to "turn aside" suggests that he turn from the "straight" road ahead, and the implications are obvious. Jael does not only suggest; she practically implores with repetition. Jael's words are provocative and sexual in connotation, but when she anticipates his possible reaction and tells him not to fear, she is giving herself away. Why would a woman who is enticing a man caution him not to fear? What does a man have to fear from a woman in these circumstances? The implication is that Jael does not have only the "sexual" circumstances she is suggesting in mind. But neither the reader nor Sisera notes the implications of her words until they become explicit in her actions.

As for Sisera, he seems to have either no choice or no qualms about going into the tent of a man who is friendly with the king he serves. He has no way of knowing that she may have an allegiance other than that of her husband. He turns aside and enters her tent. The text, even in translation, is more suggestive: "He turned aside to her into her tent."

Jael covers Sisera with a rug or fly net in the tent, which suggests that he is in a prone position, one conducive to sexual activity. According to the text, he asks for something to drink. It seems that something has been omitted, some action that took place between lying down and being covered and then requesting a drink. Biblical texts are notoriously coy about reporting sexual activity, and that between a seminomadic woman and an enemy general, even for a good purpose, is probably better suppressed as much as possible.

Sisera asks for a drink of water (4:19), but she brings him a choicer drink than the water he requests. In this passage it is milk

inducing drowsiness

that she offers, but in the poetic version (5:25) it is milk but also *hem'āh,* curds, delicious and refreshing but soporific. Offering such a drink appears to be appropriate to a good host but has a suspicious element: why would she offer a guest a drink likely to make him sleep? Significantly, she covers him once again. "And he said to her, 'Please give me a little water to drink for I am thirsty,' and she opened a skin of milk and gave him to drink, and covered him" (4:19).

The repetition of "covering" reinforces the likelihood of intervening sexual activity. Adding to the conviction is Jael's own initial implication that she has something dangerous in mind when she cautions him not to fear. What could he fear? The most likely way that a woman can physically overpower a man is when he is unconscious—asleep. Any married woman—and Jael is married—knows that males are notoriously fatigued post-coitus. I suggest that Jael has used her feminine wiles to entice and seduce Sisera in order to put him to sleep, and that she gave him *hem'āh* instead of water in order to deepen that sleep. Her plans, which Sisera should "not fear," require that he be asleep.

After Jael has covered Sisera a second time, he seeks security while he sleeps. Sisera asks Jael to act as a lookout and guard and to deny his presence should any ask: "Stand at the door of the tent, and should anyone come and ask you and says 'Is there a man here?' Then you shall say, 'There is not'" (4:20).

It would seem that a man could trust a woman with whom he has just had sexual intercourse to protect him. Men do not expect a woman to use a man as some men may use women, to their own advantage. But Jael has other plans. Like those of Deborah, Jael's actions imply gender role reversal, but on a quite different plane.

Instead of watching out for predators, "Jael the wife of Heber took a tent-peg and took a hammer in her hand and *went (in)to him* stealthily and drove the peg into his temple and she beat it into the ground (4:21, my italics).

When Jael approaches Sisera to kill him, the text uses the very phrase that is used for a male having sexual intercourse with a woman: *bô'* . . . *'el,* "come into." She "came (in) to him," just as Samson "came (in)to" his wife and a harlot (Judg 15:1; 16:1). This phrase is so explicitly identified with the sexual act that its appearance in this passage reinforces the earlier implication of sexuality.

Her beating the peg into the ground is itself suggestive of sexual activity. Can we say that Jael literally "screwed" [or: "socially /sexually abused"] Sisera? That is the implication of the text.

The last phrases of the verse, "and he had been fast asleep, and he was faint [with fatigue] and he died" (4:21c), attests to the success of Jael's strategy. The implicit threat of "do not fear" is ironically resolved with "and he died."

The narrative sequence closes with Barak chasing Sisera, only to have Jael come out of her tent to meet him. "'Come, and I will show you the man whom you are seeking.' And he *came (in)to her* and behold Sisera, fallen dead, and the peg in his temple" (4:22). When Jael goes out to meet Sisera, she is identified as Jael; otherwise merely as "she." When she kills Sisera she does so as the wife of Heber, and when she goes out to meet Barak, she is once again Jael. The text suggests that when a woman invites a man into her tent, she may be identified only as a single woman. No man's name can be identified with his wife's extramarital sexuality or even nonsexual contact with another man; but when she is about to kill, she is fortified with the name of her husband.

Once again, Jael invites a man into her tent. Jael is portrayed as proud and empowered (without feminine shame) by her deed, and when Barak enters her tent he too "is screwed" (or: "is socially/sexually abused") by Jael: note the telltale verb choice, here social and ironic rather than sexual: "came in(to) her." She has, as Deborah prophesied, conquered the man whom Barak sought. Jael has shown neither any of the hesitation of Barak nor the feminine constraints of her culture. Jael clearly acts above and beyond all the rules. The clue to the narrative—and most important—is that she acts not for her own pleasure or power but solely for the good of the Israelite people.

In this narrative, women have commanded the action to a remarkable degree. There are some interesting distinctions, however. Deborah's actions are directed by YHWH and constrained by males, particularly Barak, who must do her bidding. Deborah cannot fight her/YHWH's wars. Her actions are entirely honorable and culturally acceptable, for she never directs males as a female: she speaks as an emissary of YHWH. Jael, on the other hand, acts entirely on her own. She has no authority from above or elsewhere; she acts in ways that are forbidden—but effective—to save the people. The two women, using prophecy and sex, conquer the enemy. The dedication of Deborah and Jael is to the common good: they do nothing for self-glorification or to achieve power over others. The implicit contrast with masculine power struggles is dramatic. These audacious woman have broken all the implicit rules of biblical sexual politics, and yet tradition honors them for their actions.

Hannah: Marginalized Victim and Social Redeemer

*E*thnographic materials indicate that varying degrees of margin-alization are an effective means of social control. In the rela-tively closed society of biblical literature described in 1 Samuel, extreme marginalization, physical isolation, was stipulated for indi-viduals who demonstrated an "abnormal" physical condition or so-cial behavior, for instance menstruation, disease or anticovenantal conduct. However, not all marginalization is physical. Most individ-uals at some time or another have experienced, at least briefly, the emotional marginalization of being an "outsider," an "Other" in specific situations.

This emotional marginalization is a significant component of the narrative of Hannah (1 Samuel 1). Each of the three individuals with whom Hannah interacts—her rival wife, Peninnah, her hus-band, Elkanah, and the priest, Eli—contributes to her emotional marginalization in a different way. The motives for and methods of marginalization used by each of the characters comment upon the social milieu even as they delineate interpersonal relationships and character.

Hannah is the loved but barren wife of a man who has two wives—a familiar motif in the Hebrew Bible. Sarah is barren when Hagar conceives, and even when he has fathered a son by Hagar, Abraham puts Hagar at Sarah's disposition, confirming which wife he loves.[1] Rachel, the beloved of Jacob, is also barren while Leah bears him many sons. In traditional readings, all three fruitful wives

provoke the barren but loved ones—Sarah, Rachel and Hannah—
thus increasing their suffering.

In the Hebrew Bible women are usually portrayed as jealous of
each other. Indeed, jealousy and seductiveness are the chief transgressions projected upon women.[2] In narrative depictions of men
the chief male transgressions are theft, intrigue, rape and murder.
Nevertheless, it is not clear that such masculine behavior is necessarily recognized as transgressions; see, for instance, the aftermath
of the rape of Dinah (Genesis 34). The text may just suggest that
"men are like that." We may regard analogously the persistent narrative stance on feminine jealousy, which has the text imply that
"women are like that."

A convenient tool for exploring jealousy in the context of biblical Hebrew narrative is offered by René Girard's concept of
"mimetic desire." Girard coined this term for the complex of attitudes and actions arising from imitation of another generated by
desire of what the other has. This acquisitive mimetic desire thus
subsumes jealousy, rivalry and all the actions taken to gain the object of desire.[3] Such conflictual and destructive mimesis is a disruptive force and must be subjected to social constraints; there must be
a "'normal' mechanism to interrupt and reverse" its disordering effects.[4] Without social control of rivalry, it can escalate into reciprocal forms and gather sufficient strength to destroy the social unit's
functional entity. Although the term "mimetic desire" usually refers
to this acquisitive form, desire may also be expressed in 'non-ac-
quisitive forms—those that are good to imitate'.[5] Although mimetic
desire is part of human nature, we are not necessarily at its mercy;
the acquisitive form can be deliberately bridled and not allowed to
generate social conflict.

In its acquisitive form, mimetic desire is directed toward an object that the subject desires *"because the rival desires it"*[6] (author's
emphasis). To imitate the desires of someone else is to turn this
someone else into a rival as well as a model. Of the three entities—
subject (the one desiring an object), rival (the one who is in possession) and the object of desire—Girard accords the rival the
dominant role because the rival's desiring an object "alerts the subject to the desirability of the object."[7] It follows that two desires

converging on the same object are bound to clash;[8] therefore, uncontrolled mimesis coupled with desire necessarily involves conflict. Furthermore, once the possessor—rival realizes that what he or she has is desirable, it becomes more valuable, and he or she becomes zealous to retain it. Should the desiring subject attain the coveted object, the positions are reversed: the former rival in turn assumes the position of desiring subject in order to regain the object. With reciprocal exchange, mimetic desire and its attendant violence spread, potentially to engulf the social order.

The prevalent cultural accommodation to mimetic desire, the focus of Girard's work, occurs in cultures that channel mimetic desire as sacrifice, a safe outlet within the society that thereby protects the society from dissolution. The sacrificial victim is an individual who has, by some means or other, demonstrated difference but who is innocent of the charges, thereby first an Other, then a victim. By projecting the social ills of both sides (subject and rival) onto the innocent but different individual, and by sacrificing this Other, the society maintains social cohesion, at least for the moment.

Literary and sociological evidence suggests, however, that the social groups reflected in biblical literature were directed to govern the basic human impulse of acquisitive mimetic desire by *exposing* it as such within the social group, lest it disrupt the culture; and, if necessary, by *displacing* it outside the social group, with foreign social groups it regards as "evil" or dangerous.[9] Marshall Sahlins describes

> the tribal plan ... as a series of more and more inclusive kinship-residential sectors. . . . The close kinsmen who render assistance are particularly near kinsmen in a spatial sense: it is in regard to people of the household, the camp, hamlet, or village that compassion in required, inasmuch as interaction is intense and *peaceable solidarity essential.*[10]

Under the circumstances described by Sahlins, striving toward social solidarity, which implies rejection of mimetic desire within the intimate social group, is characteristic of primitive social organizations. Such communities typically take pains to maintain cohesive and harmonic social unity, beginning with the family.

Within the household, pooling of goods and services makes necessities available to all, eliminating differentiation of members "in favor of the coherence of the whole"; it is "the *constituting activity* of a group."[11] Kinship is a social aspect of mutual aid, and generosity, not competitive pricing, effects material exchanges.[12] This is obvious even in contemporary households: parents do not charge their children, other relatives, or guests for food.

The Hebrew Bible, although it recognizes sacrifice and the sacrificial crisis, does not accept them as necessary. Unlike the literature of sacrificial societies, the Bible does not seek to hide the workings of mimetic desire. It does the opposite: it directs attention to the negative aspects of mimetic desire (jealousy and violence), often by displacement of the sacrificial victim, exposing the misunderstood "necessity" of sacrifice in order to thwart human sacrifice. There is no denial that sacrifice, often displaced as animal sacrifice, played an important role in the evolving biblical community, but biblical literature discloses that this group sought to reject *human* sacrifice within the community as an unavoidable consequence of mimetic desire. But mimetic desire is, according to Girard, part of human nature. It may be displaced, but it is not nullified. Even though individuals may not be sacrificed, they may still be victimized through the effects of mimetic desire.

The Hebrew Bible consistently exposes individuals who are controlled by mimetic desire, that is, imitating another by desiring what the other has.[13] Indeed, the Ten Commandments are specific stipulations against various forms of mimetic desire, so that acquisitive mimetic desire is essentially anticovenantal.[14] But two women married to one man are repeatedly depicted in a reciprocal exchange of mimetic desire: they both wish to be fertile and (most) loved. Each woman makes the Other a model and rival; each is jealous (desires what the Other has) and zealous (desires to retain what the Self has) at the same time. In fact, the word most used for "second wife," *ṣārah*, means a female "rival" or "foe" or "opponent," the feminine form of the masculine *ṣar*, "enemy" (with all the implications retained in the feminine form). Thus the language conveys (and thereby shapes) the expected behavior of two women who share a husband even though that behavior is disparaged by the social norms. Masculine mimetic desire is displaced onto the female.

With such displacement, it is understandable that female rejection of mimetic desire occurs only once in the Hebrew Bible. This is unexpected in a social structure where kinship status is demonstrated by forms of etiquette, where reciprocity and cooperation determine the economic aspects of domestic decisions, all aimed at "maintaining domestic contentment."[15] In such a social organization it is singular that the women, at the center of household life, are not shown in any acts of reciprocal generosity.

Hannah, who is the rival wife to Peninnah, refuses to enter into the subject-rival competition and is victimized. The rival wife's actions draw attention to Hannah as an Other—a barren woman in a society that valorizes fertility—which Hannah experiences as a "torment." If Peninnah is jealous because Elkanah loves Hannah, if she is using Hannah's lack of fertility to attract Elkanah's love for herself, then Peninnah's mimetic desire is the basis of Hannah's being emotionally marginalized in this quarter, despite the narrator's observation that YHWH had closed Hannah's womb. In other words, Peninnah is exploiting YHWH's action (his closing of Hannah's womb) by responding to mimetic desire—contrary to YHWH's commandments and the social code.[16] With masculine mimetic desire ostensibly displaced onto the females, Elkanah initially appears as a nonmimetic "norm" for his rival wives.

In the social structure described in the Hebrew Bible several women might stand in a variety of relationships to a man. The primary relationship is usually with an *'iššāh*, "wife"; and some men have several wives without any further distinction between them. A woman may also be a *šiphhāh*, "handmaid," usually to a wife; a *pilegeš* (or even more indelicately, *lᵉhenah*), "concubine" to the husband; or a female slave. Peninnah is defined as none of these. She is a second wife, a *ṣārah*. Peninnah is an opponent-foe-rival wife because this word has been selected to describe her; this does not mean that she is any of these for Hannah. Notably, Hannah never shows any envy of Peninnah. Hannah wants a child, but she does not project her desire onto Peninnah. Nothing in the text suggests that Hannah wants a child because Peninnah has children or because Peninnah taunts her. Hannah's desire arises from within and is maintained as a personal, as yet unfulfilled wish.

Under the circumstances of the 1 Samuel 1 narrative, Hannah's need to bear children according to the precepts of this culture suggests that she does not take the cultural prescriptions lightly. Accordingly, she must be thoroughly familiar with the cultural disdain of mimetic desire. Although Hannah suffers Peninnah's torments, there is no suggestion that she seeks to gain revenge, that is, to generate reciprocal mimetic desire. In this tale of feminine jealousy, Hannah shows no jealousy; by keeping her desire to herself, she does not express it mimetically, acquisitively. Desire remains introspective for this woman; it is a *good* mimetic desire. Hannah desires to have what women have, a child; she does not desire to have a child because Peninnah has children. She does not perpetrate masculine displacement of mimetic desire on the female, and she proves herself an Israelite observant of the covenantal strictures. There is, however, no feminine bonding depicted; Peninnah's mimetic desire obviates that possibility. Hannah is marginalized as a childless Other in a culture where a woman's purpose in life is depicted as reproduction and associated tasks.

Elkanah, as a devout Israelite, may be assumed to be familiar with the narratives of Israelite history, including explicit as well as implicit statements of masculine rejection of mimetic desire. He must also know about Sarah and Hagar, about Leah and Rachel; in fact, Elkanah may think his experience of female jealousy is buttressed by those biblical narratives. After all, the language reinforces jealousy among second wives: they are "enemy-rival-wives."

Perhaps that is the reason Elkanah seeks to advance Hannah's personal desire for a child as mimetic desire (her wanting what Peninnah has) and thereby elicit jealousy between his wives. He gives portions of sacrifice to each member of his family and thus differentiates between the two women in terms of their fruitfulness. That Peninnah's tormenting Hannah is associated with Elkanah's portion-giving is implied by the sequence of the narrative. Even though Peninnah and Hannah are introduced and contrasted in terms of fruitfulness in 1:2, Peninnah's tormenting Hannah is not mentioned until immediately *after* Elkanah's giving of the portions; and the association of motherhood and torment is supported by the following line: "And her rival wife really provoked her, to irritate her because YHWH had closed her womb" (1:6). Elkanah reinforces

Peninnah's advantageous status at the sacrifice, and Peninnah "rubs it in."

The action is summarized as an annual event: "And so *he* [Elkanah] *did* year by year; as often as *she* [Hannah] went up to the house of yhwh *she* [Peninnah] provoked *her* [Hannah]" (1:7). Elkanah assigns portions; when Hannah goes to the house of yhwh, Peninnah provokes her. There is no suggestion of Peninnah's hostility during the rest of the year or at least no suggestion that it is intense; the antagonism seems exacerbated by the visit to the temple at Shiloh and Elkanah's portion-giving that is associated with that visit.

Elkanah's sense of justice apparently demands that he give equal portions to each member of his family: nevertheless, he gives one— a generous one—to Hannah,[17] one to Peninnah, his second wife, and one to each of the latter's sons and daughters (1:4). This public display of difference—and it is *difference* that marks the victim—is augmented by provocations from Peninnah, Hannah's rival wife, year after year. Elkanah's actions exacerbate disharmony in his family even though biblical literature suggests other, less divisive ways of being just. Elkanah could have learned from Joseph, who gave each of his brothers by Leah a portion of food, of clothing and of gold; but Benjamin, a brother of his own mother, Rachel, he gave five times as much, so that each group of mothers' sons received an equal portion (Gen. 43:34). In so doing, Joseph honored the mothers equally, whether or not that was his primary intention.

Now Hannah has no children, but to honor his wives equally Elkanah could give his wives equal portions; that is, one to each of the children and their mother, and an equivalent number of portions to Hannah, so that the women would be equal in their shares. Elkanah gives Hannah only one portion, but one *generous* portion (1:6); his inconsistency draws attention to his restricting of Hannah's portion and enlarging it at the same time, neither of which is a comfort to Hannah. This annually repeated disparity in his portion-giving and its equally repeated consequence in Peninnah's provocations of Hannah suggest that his experience of the women as jealous of one another—over him—is not altogether discomfiting to him. The one woman (Peninnah) wants his love, the other (Hannah) his children. Elkanah seems to aid and abet strife between the women.

One must question Elkanah's motives in his interactions with his wives. It seems that the generation of mimetic desire in this narrative does not arise from the two women but from Elkanah. Insofar as they identify themselves with their reproductive functions, Hannah and Peninnah are types of the women Esther Fuchs says are created "in the image of patriarchal desire."[18] By fostering mimetic desire between the women Elkanah may be displacing his own discontent, his desire for a son from the woman he loves. As a result, the women in strife become a foil for Elkanah's apparent "purity."

According to Jung, such a projection cannot occur without a "hook"; in other words, it must be feasible in the situation described. It is certainly possible that a barren woman be jealous of a fertile one, but equally likely that she *not* be jealous, especially in a society that valorizes repudiation of envy and emphasizes generosity and cohesiveness within the family unit. The women could comfort and console each other, even closing ranks as women against the male Other. Displacing his frustrated desire for a child by Hannah, Elkanah projects mimetic desire between the two women and thereby initiates a divide-and-conquer tactic with the women in his household.

Hannah does not rise to the bait. The unfulfilled desire that Elkanah projects outward on others Hannah keeps for herself and turns inward. She refuses mimetic desire and concentrates on her own desire: she internalizes her pain by weeping and not eating, and by speaking her heart out to one whom she believes will listen. Between Peninnah and Elkanah, both of whom project their mimetic desires on her, Hannah is an example of what James G. Williams calls a "marginal" female, "different to the point of being *too* different."[19]

Hannah is addressed by two men: her husband Elkanah, and the priest Eli. Both these men are presented as admirable. Elkanah appears with full genealogy as an Ephraimite who lives in the Ephraimite territory (1:1) and practices religious devotion: he goes to sacrifice at the altar at Shiloh annually (1:3). All of these attributes endorse the virtuousness of the individual. Eli the priest may be inferred to be righteous as an attribute of his position. But, as often happens in the Hebrew Bible, these initial impressions give way to ambiguity as the narrative develops. In fact, both of these men are so involved with their own perceptions that they fail to comprehend a suffering woman, a woman who is wife to the first and a devotee of the temple of YHWH to the second.

Elkanah is described as loving Hannah (1:8). That his love is current and not in the past is attested by the Hebrew syntax.[20] However, such a rare, bald statement of love from a presumably reliable narrator is confounded by Elkanah's "conversation" with Hannah. In his speech to her, Elkanah notes that Hannah weeps and does not eat. His response is to cajole her: "Hannah, why do you weep? And why do you not eat? And why is your heart morose? Am I not more to you than ten sons?" (1:8). Elkanah's "consoling" of Hannah does not allow her time to answer his initial questions, which would effect communication between husband and wife, but would also draw him into involvement. That his questions are rhetorical and thus not intended to probe Hannah's situation is evident from their quick succession. While they do not allow Hannah to convey her thoughts or feelings, Elkanah's questions do relinquish some tacit information about him. His questions are typical of what psycholinguist Virginia Satir classifies as the "Blamer Mode." Such speakers "don't bother about an answer; that is unimportant. The blamer is much more interested in throwing weight around than really finding out anything."[21] Elkanah is depicted as imposing himself without regard for the Other, who happens to be his suffering wife.

Furthermore, these questions also reveal that Elkanah, as typical of a "blamer," "longs to be connected."[22] His last question, "Am I not more to you than ten sons?" expresses this desire in a formulation that precludes an answer, thereby making overtures toward connection even as he closes off the possibility. Only with this question does Elkanah allow time for Hannah's answer, which she wisely forfeits.

Significantly, Elkanah's third question uses a form of the word r', which means "morose" or "unsatisfied" when it refers to countenance or heart, as it does here, but primarily means "evil" or "destructive." The stronger implications are usually ignored in translations, which ameliorates Elkanah's judgment of his wife and thus alters the relationship to Hannah depicted by the narrative.[23] In the Hebrew one hears "evil" even as one understands "morose," "unsatisfied."

Notably, Elkanah's consoling judgment of Hannah is followed by *his* claim for love, which I paraphrase as, "is not your love for me greater than your desire for even ten sons?" Elkanah does not comfort his wife with his love *for her.* As a male, Elkanah does not have his entire existence connected to procreation as the female Hannah is supposed to do in the patriarchal culture. He has already fathered sons and daughters; his responsibility for generation has been fulfilled. Although his frustration suggests that he wants children by the woman he loves, he apparently "loves" Hannah without regard for the need she has, as a woman in this culture, to bear children. His suggestion that he is more than "ten sons" makes light of her deprivation as it attempts to equate conjugal love with parental love.

Furthermore, all of Elkanah's questions to Hannah fall under the psycholinguistic category of verbal attacks. The first three are in the "Blamer Mode" under the disguise of affectionate concern, and the fourth hides the attack under a presupposition—that Elkanah's love is "worth more than" the love of ten sons.[24] The skilled attacker may bury verbal abuse under surface signals of tenderness and affection, claiming tender loving care for which the recipient should be grateful, but in fact the recipient will more likely be burdened with a second layer of hurt, which leads to confused misery and confusing guilt. Elkanah ostensibly tries to diminish Hannah's suffering by attempting to show that it is unjustified, claiming that her love for him is more valuable than "ten sons"; in fact, he increases it. When Hannah is not granted the dignity of her suffering, she suffers even more. Elkanah's use of these modes of verbal attack discloses a man who is threatening, angry and punishing beneath the surface. He typically directs his anger at the weakest target, in this case Hannah.

Elkanah's use of verbal attack supports the claim that he is frustrated because the woman he loves is barren. It is psychologically understandable that he unloads his anger on the object of his frustration, especially since she is the weakest target available. In an interesting twist, Elkanah does not suffer from mimetic desire; there is no "object" he wishes to take from someone else. However, his actions instigate mimetic desire between his two wives. A foil for Hannah's nonmimetic handling of her own inner desire, Elkanah is betrayed by his mode of speech as well as his deeds. Hannah, even

though she is rival to Peninnah and object to Elkanah, is an innocent victim.

It is clear that Elkanah assumes dominance in his "conversation"
with Hannah by taking the first "turn" and by establishing the
topic—and this is all well and good.[25] But Elkanah abuses his dominance by asking questions without allowing an answer three times,
and by concluding with a question that cannot be answered. He
thus maintains the first and last word, destroying any possibility of
verbal exchange and effectively maintaining dominance. As long as
Hannah is wife but not mother, Elkanah marginalizes her through
verbal attack and renders her speechless.

Later (1:21-23), when Hannah is no longer in a socially weak position, Elkanah's manner of speech to her is entirely different. Hannah initiates the conversation and establishes the topic. She, unlike
Elkanah, does not verbally attack; and she allows her husband
ample opportunity to answer. Hannah's conflict-avoiding behavior
is, according to linguist Deborah Tannen, typically female: "To most
women, conflict is a threat to connection," and women struggle "to
keep the ties strong . . . and accommodate to others' needs while
making what efforts they can at damage control with respect to
their own needs and preferences."[26] Male focus on status, hierarchy
and rank allows Elkanah to attack Hannah under the guise of protection (domination); with female focus on interdependence, Hannah *expects* her actions to be influenced by others.[27] She has no need
to suppress Elkanah's response. On the other hand, Elkanah's verbal
aggression in 1:8 is typical of the male: "male behavior typically en-
tails contest. . . . Furthermore, oral performance in self-display is
part of a larger framework in which many men approach life as a
contest."[28]

After the birth of her son, Hannah does not go up to make the
annual offering at the house of the Lord. She wishes to remain at
home until her son is weaned, at which time she brings him to
abide at the temple, as she promised (1:24-28). She sends her husband off with her "rival" (1:21-22a), clearly demonstrating that she
harbors no jealousy. Hannah's remaining at home also interrupts
the pattern of provocation established by her husband's portion-
giving. In contrast to Hannah's sure knowledge of what she will do

is Elkanah's response, which closes with the weak "only, may the Lord establish his word" (1:23). And when she does bring Samuel to Shiloh, Hannah brings her own provisions: "a three-year-old bull, an ephah of flour, and a skin of wine" (1:24). Hannah has extricated herself from Elkanah's disruptive and isolating conduct.

Hannah's experience with Eli is hardly better. Like Elkanah, Eli judges Hannah—this time explicitly—before she can say a word: Eli's questions are in the simple "Blamer Mode," without any over-laid and contradicting emotional element; they are neither rhetori-cal nor a trap for self-incrimination. Hannah does respond, and her words constitute the climax of this part of the narrative. In the structure of her response, Hannah almost literally centers her words on the most significant aspect of her visit to the temple: "I have been pouring out my soul before YHWH" (1:15c).[29] The phrase she uses, "pouring out," is suggestive of the male part in a sexual encounter; despite her deprived existence, Hannah appears the stronger, the "male," and "pours out" her soul to God. Her conception shortly thereafter attests to the success of her plea. Eli's response is so non-specific and impersonal that it cannot be considered significant in her change from barrenness to fertility (1:17). Like Elkanah, Eli speaks from a verbal protective barrier and maintains distance.

It is curious that Eli immediately presumes that Hannah is drunk (1:13-14). Other conditions could as easily explain her be-havior: she could be a habitual lip-mover, one who "mouths" ideas unconsciously; she could "mouth" her prayers consciously, the bet-ter to communicate; she could be in grief, as indeed she is. Mere "mouthing" seems insufficient evidence for the unquestioned judg-ment Eli makes. When his presumption proves utterly false, Eli fails to accept responsibility for his misjudgment; instead, he utters easy platitudes that could apply to any person, any prayer. Hannah is judged abnormal (drunken) and thereby marginalized, and this by a man to whom she has not turned, a man who unjustly criticizes her with the authority of his position.

Hannah's independent resolution of her inner turmoil, so that she eats (there is no mention of drink) and "her countenance was no longer" (1:18) is followed by Elkanah's "knowing" Hannah and her conception.[30]

Elkanah and Eli attend to superficial "ritual" aspects of belief without perceiving deeper significances that lie in human relationships to one another and to YHWH. Hannah, although she receives the brunt of Peninnah's mimetic desire, is never shown in active reciprocity. Hannah clearly wishes to have children as Peninnah does, but, despite provocation, the text does not demonstrate any projecting, acting out or other demonstrations of envy on her part. It is Hannah who evolves as the social ideal, despite projection of mimetic desire on her by Elkanah and Peninnah and judgment of her by both Elkanah and Eli.

According to James G. Williams, "In those tales where the woman acts only for the sake of the hero or the man's world, she is a persona on the boundary, a mediator who may quickly become a victim."[31] Not interacting in any roles in the subject-rival-object triangle of mimetic desire, Hannah becomes its victim. However, because Hannah does *not* respond to mimetic desire, she is able to curtail mimetic interaction in the entire family and lead it to a more socially acceptable interaction. Hannah is a woman in a boundary situation, a situation "where the woman, by virtue of her very tenuous, sometimes marginal status, can lead the male . . . over the threshold into a safer or better zone for his survival and success."[32] She is a social redeemer.

Finally, Hannah only speaks her heart to, and is only heard by, YHWH. Her marginalization in the world of men, of human power, is emphasized by Elkanah's failure to let her speak and Eli's failure to respond meaningfully to her emotional appeal. She is also marginalized in the world of women by Peninnah's uncontrolled jealousy, repeatedly precipitated by Elkanah's actions. YHWH's hearing of Hannah attests to the fact that YHWH listens to the heart, and that of female as well as male. Hannah's meaningful relationship with YHWH overrides all human marginalization, which happens to be consistently related to anticovenantal, acquisitive mimetic desire. This narrative shows that a woman can reach YHWH by opening her heart when males, even powerful men like Elkanah and priests like Eli, may project their own weaknesses on the "weaker" women or be absorbed in empty ritual. And although Elkanah and Eli project Hannah as diminished (by Elkanah as morose, with implications of evil; by Eli as drunk), her strength of character and integrity of belief finally render *her* the noble core of the narrative, and both Elkanah and Eli as ambiguous by comparison. The narrative describes victimization of an innocent, and victim reversal, so that Hannah evolves from an Other into a paradigm, a model of woman, and redeems her family from mimetic desire.

And the rival wife? Her jealousy and mimetic desire (she is zealous for the motherhood Hannah is expected to be jealous of) serve as a foil for Hannah's refusal of mimetic desire. In this respect Hannah seems to resist "biblical sexual politics."[33] The implicit traditional interpretation of women as jealous of each other in opposition to the explicit cultural and religious mores suggests, perhaps, the magnitude of the threat of female bonding to the patriarchal system. But even Hannah desires a *son* (not a *child*, or a *daughter*), and the narrative depicts her as relinquishing the joys of parenthood, thus limiting her function to reproduction and nursing, the biologically programmed aspects of being a female. Hannah refuses the mimetic desire and envy despised in the patriarchal culture but displaced upon women; at the same time, the desires she achieves are those ascribed to women in the patriarchal system. Victim and redeemer, Hannah reinforces the patriarchal image of women.

Bathsheba Revealed

*A*lthough she is the mother of Solomon, regarded in the Hebrew Bible and in some critical traditions as the greatest monarch of the Israelite people, Bathsheba is relatively neglected in commentary. She is not mentioned (except as the object of David's desire) in a study on the monarchic period, even when the subject is the "Matriarchate and Hebrew Regal Succession."[1] Adele Berlin views Bathsheba in her introductory appearance as "a complete non-person. She is not even a minor character, but simply part of the plot."[2] Commentators take little note of Bathsheba's feelings—or David's—"despite the fact that powerful and deep emotions play a crucial role" in the seduction scene (2 Samuel 11).[3] In sum, Bathsheba as an individual, as a woman, scarcely exists in the Hebrew Bible and in biblical interpretation, and even then almost exclusively through the lens of male perception.

It is male perception that introduces Bathsheba and the central plot conflict (2 Samuel 11): David sees her bathing as he walks on the roof of the palace in the evening. He sends for her, and she becomes pregnant by him as a result of one sexual encounter—while still married to another man. Her husband Uriah, a Hittite soldier in the king's army, is away at war, which presents a delicate situation.

The text is ambiguous about Bathsheba's role: in commentary, she is generally polarized as either a temptress, bathing on her roof to catch David's attention,[4] or as an innocent victim of David's lust.[5] Mieke Bal suggests that ironic ambiguity "prevents the reader from making more specific interpretations."[6] Provocatively, the text does not hold Bathsheba accountable for the adultery, while blame is heaped on David.[7]

While the seduction scene is meager (and the child of lust dies), it does eventuate in Bathsheba's becoming the mother of a king; and she is the third woman identified as a mother to royal lineage in biblical texts. Tamar (Gen 38:13-26) and Ruth are identified as ancestral mothers of kings, and their stories suggest parallels that amplify the little we know about Bathsheba.[8]

The Gap in the Text

Bathsheba is first seen as an object—a beautiful woman who is bathing. An unknown "someone" in David's court identifies her to David through her male relationships (father and husband). Bathsheba the individual is recognized as pedigreed (of an important family), beautiful and bathing. Her bathing—purifying herself, as Meir Sternberg has made us aware—indicates she has completed her menses and, therefore, is not pregnant.[9] We note that Bathsheba is bathing in the evening, when she could be seen, rather than in the obscurity of the night.

In this scene, David's association with active verbs, particularly his repeated exercise of "send" (*šlḥ*), marks his command of the situation. Bathsheba, though she is the object of male actions—she "is taken" (from *lqḥ*) by the servant and David lays with her—is not utterly passive; she "comes" (from *bw'*) to David.[10] Noting that Bathsheba's arrival and sexual involvement are fully covered without the phrase, "and she came to him," the reader is alerted to excess verbiage, bordering on redundancy, which demands attention. The superfluous words do serve to mitigate Bathsheba's passivity, to be sure; and the use of "come," with its connotations of sexuality, insinuates Bathsheba's complicity in the sexual adventure. From Bathsheba's point of view, her complicity with the king's wishes may be regarded as her attempt to bear a child rather than merely participation in an adulterous (lustful) act.

The end of the encounter mentions purification by Bathsheba once again: "And David sent messengers and took her and she came to him and he lay with her and she purified herself from her uncleanness and she returned to her house" (2 Sam 11:4, literal translation).

Bathsheba's purification at this juncture is usually interpreted as referring to her earlier purification: "David sent messengers to fetch her; she came to him and he lay with her—she had just purified herself after her period—and she went back home" (JPS). "So David sent messengers, and took her; and she came to him, and he lay with her. (Now she was purifying herself from her uncleanness.)" (RSV).

Two words are critical: "purified" and "uncleanness." The Hebrew *mitqaddešet* is the Hithpael participle (singular, feminine) of *qdš*; extending the meaning to "set apart," it denotes "to consecrate oneself by purification, of priests and Levites, and of woman."[11] The second word, *miṭṭum'āthāh*, "from her uncleanness" from *ṭm'h*, "uncleanness," usually refers to sexual or to ethical and religious uncleanness. These encompass a range of ritual uncleanness of men and of women's uncleanness resulting from copulation and menstruation.[12] There is just one narrative instance of "ritual uncleanness" of woman: that of Bathsheba, in this verse. The initial reference to Bathsheba's purifying herself does not mention her "uncleanness"; it states only that she is bathing. Although 11:4 can be interpreted as referring to her earlier purification from her menses, it seems an awkward reading. I suggest Bathsheba's second purification may be from her sexual and ethical uncleanness. In any case, whether this purification is understood to reiterate Bathsheba's earlier ritual or to reflect her purifying herself a second time, after the sexual act, the sexual act *concludes* with emphasis on Bathsheba's *purification*. In this reading, the repetition of "purification" at this juncture in the text hints at Bathsheba's motive—not desire for a sexual romp but desire for motherhood. With "purification," her complicity in unethical behavior is absolved. This reading justifies Bathsheba's vindication in the text and subsequent commentary.

Bathsheba has no voice before or during the sexual encounter. David's voice, while not quoted directly, is conveyed through the mission he directs: He *sends* someone to inquire; he *sends* messengers to get her. Only when her body has "spoken" does Bathsheba demonstrate command of the situation. The sudden burst of four verbs associated with Bathsheba contrasts with her earlier docile silence. Her first action is *conception:* her body acts. The conception gives her power to send, as previously David repeatedly *sent:* Bathsheba acts. With sending, she has voice and *speaks.* Bathsheba's two words constitute the first direct speech in the narrative, and her words are directed to the king. To this point, David has spoken only indirectly, but Bathsheba tells; she speaks directly.[13] Finally, Bathsheba's speaking is emphasized with yet another reference to speech: her speech is announced when she "says" to David, "I [am] pregnant" (11:5).

This sequence suggests that conception gives woman power, perhaps power beyond that of the male. Woman's body can speak and give woman speech.[14] Furthermore, the woman's speech initiates male response. David's authority, with repeated verbs of action—sending people here and there—is subtly undermined by the woman, for the balance of action in the narrative is in response to Bathsheba's two words of direct speech: "I [am] pregnant." Of course, Bathsheba's words are the result of David's sending for her; but if, as I suggest, Bathsheba is complicit in the sexual encounter, she is less the object than is readily apparent.

Although the reader cannot discern the tone of Bathsheba's words, they are baldly direct: there is no hedging or apology or humble appeal to the king. These are not the words of an intimidated woman, although we are to suppose her seduction by the king involves intimidation. The king does not entice Bathsheba with seductive words; he "sends" for her and "takes" her. David's actions presume the privileges of power, which depend upon subordinates being intimidated by that power. It is possible that Bathsheba is initially intimidated but becomes self-confident once she acquires the power of pregnancy. Another possibility, which does not invoke this dramatic change of personality, is that Bathsheba has not been intimidated at any point. If Bathsheba is not intimidated, has Bathsheba been "taken," or has David?

Bathsheba's words are the only words of direct speech by either of the main characters to one another until David is old and approaching death. David speaks indirectly to a nameless "someone" and sends nameless messengers, actions that may be perceived as symbolic of David's indirect, unethical actions. Ironically, David later speaks directly to Bathsheba's husband, urging him to go home and wash his feet.[15] He also sends a "gift" after Uriah.[16] David's intention is clearly that Uriah sleep with his wife Bathsheba and relieve David of a difficult situation.

But Uriah does not go home. He lies down at the entrance of the king's house. Uriah "lay," *wayyiškab*, alone, exactly as David "lay," *wayyiškab*, with Bathsheba earlier—but Uriah's action ironically *opposes* the king's wishes. Both Bathsheba and Uriah respond to the king's orders in a manner overtly passive but in fact active: Bathsheba acquiesces to orders she may herself have precipitated; Uriah resists. Uriah's refusal suggests it is not necessary to accede to the king's orders—at least for a man. It may be another question as to whether a woman can refuse the king—if she wants to—even if the order is sexual and immoral.[17]

The text has led the reader to surmise that Bathsheba is not pregnant when she sleeps with David; since no mention is made of children, it may be assumed that she has never conceived. No hint is offered as to how long Bathsheba has been a married woman, without conception; yet she conceives as a result of one sexual encounter with David. Typically, biblical narratives assume the problem with failure to conceive is that of the woman; I know of no narrative text that even acknowledges the possibility of male infertility. Sarah, Hannah, Rachel all conceive after long periods of infertility—with the help of (a male) God; and each of those narratives supports the fact of male fertility (hence female infertility) with a secondary woman who becomes pregnant by the same husband. It seems that male sterility among the Israelites is not to be countenanced. However, it is possible that Bathsheba's husband may implicitly be permitted infertility since he is, after all, a Hittite. Faithful as he is to the Israelites, his patrimony is different. Perhaps, in this narrative, not all males of other races are as virile as the Israelites.[18]

David's object in the liaison is clear: lust.[19] Bathsheba, however, may not be merely the passive object of his lust.[20] If she has been married to an infertile man, warrior though he is, she may find it necessary to mate with another male to fulfill her biological and social function as a woman—to become a mother. Granted, she may not have known where the infertility lay—with her or her husband—but her failure to conceive is no doubt of great concern to her. As a married woman, she cannot test her capacity for reproduction outside her marital bonds; but if the king commands her, she has the pretext of excuse. Bathsheba can accept the king's order and at the same time fulfill her mission: to bear sons.

Provocatively, the text leaves ambiguous the circumstances of Bathsheba's ritual bathing. Has Bathsheba regularly bathed on her roof? In this scenario, David may be aware of the beautiful woman whose husband is now in the field, and David makes his move. Or is this the first time Bathsheba has bathed on the roof, potentially in view of the king? In this perspective, she has chosen to purify herself there now, when her husband is in the field and she is again not pregnant. The text does not suggest that David's walking on his roof was motivated by any ulterior motives; on the contrary, David's spontaneity—in walking and seeing and taking—reinforces Bathsheba's maneuver in bathing on her roof *at this time*. I suggest Bathsheba may well have been purifying herself on her roof with the hope of seducing King David into "seducing" her.

In this light, Bathsheba may knowingly "come" to the king in the hope of conceiving without renouncing her honor. In the social context of this narrative, women usually achieve honor by preserving their positive "shame"—by deference and submission to male authority—and by the status accorded motherhood. In this reading, Bathsheba seeks the honor associated with motherhood instead of accepting its opposite, social discrimination as a barren woman. She risks a single "shameless" incident of sexual infidelity—forbidden for women—in order to achieve lasting honor as a mother.[21] But Bathsheba avoids the sexual autonomy forbidden women. She acts in deference and submission to male authority. Bathsheba's purification before—and especially after—the act reinforces the ethical aspect of the encounter for her. Female-initiated seduction (viz. Ruth) or adultery (see Tamar [Gen 38:13-26]) may be textually regarded as righteous if the action answers to a good cause—and for a biblical woman, that cause is procreation.[22] Bathsheba continues the paradigm established by her female predecessors: women as mothers in the royal lineage.

Woman as Mother

Childbearing was a social function in ancient Israel, and fecundity, barrenness, and the loss of children were of urgent concern to men, women, and the nation.[23]

I propose that Bathsheba's desire for motherhood causes her to exploit her sexual allure as a temptress in order to gain her objective, which involves adultery with the king; yet her actions are excused by the implied narrator. Significantly, Bathsheba is never considered a temptress by biblical commentators; "the temptress in biblical literature is a figure of the strange, alien, shadowy 'other' in which one may lose one's bearings, one's sense of order."[24] Bathsheba is not "other"—she is descended from an important Israelite family but she does cause David to lose his bearings. A temptress, furthermore, "portrays one who mediates a destiny contrary to the divine purpose," and Bathsheba's desire to become a mother, in this reading, is utterly consistent with the divine purpose.[25] In any case, "biblical stories do not draw up an absolute, clear-cut line of separation between the temptress and Israel's heroines."[26] Bathsheba presents a subtle opportunity for enticement rather than an overt sexual invitation.

Phyllis Bird observes that "The two most common images of woman in the historical writings are those of wife and mother,"[27] yet there was a gulf between these two roles. The wife was such as almost invisible; the wife who was childless (presumed barren) was a reproach in Israel: she was derided by other women, her role as wife was threatened, and she was denied the honor identified with being a mother. Motherhood offered the highest status for women and, more than honor, it brought security through the approval of husband and community. Motherhood also "offered the woman her only opportunity to exercise legitimate power over another person. . . . The only relationship in which dominance by the woman was sanctioned was the mother-child relationship."[28] For Bathsheba, motherhood, especially with the king as father to her child, is a means for advancing her standing in the community. Bathsheba's purpose—motherhood—and the divine orders to humans—generation—are one and the same.

Paradigm as Gap-Replenisher

This reading of Bathsheba's actions offers interesting correspondences with those of her predecessors as foremothers in the Davidic lineage: the very same Tamar and Ruth alluded to earlier. Significantly, all three tales of female predecessors of kings are highly sexual in content and exhibit women as initiators of sexual encounters. Tamar (Gen 38:13-26), we recall, seduces her father-in-law by presenting herself as a veiled prostitute in order to conceive when Judah's youngest son has been withheld from her. Ruth, childless and widowed, uncovers Boaz's feet on the threshing floor; and he understands her intent (Ruth 3:1-14). Bathsheba bathes where she is visible from the roof of the king's house, a favorite place to walk in the evening (2 Sam 11:2). All these female ancestors/mothers of kings know they want motherhood, and they take action to make sure they conceive. To do so, they use their beauty to arouse the sexual desire that excites males: they make themselves the object of male desire but exhibit no sexual desire themselves.

These encounters may involve deception, as Tamar disguises herself as a prostitute (Gen 38:12-19); and Ruth steals into the threshing floor under the cloak of darkness, when Boaz is asleep, to lie down at his feet (Ruth 3:1-14). In a biblical twist, Bathsheba's story turns the deception from the female to the male, to David, who attempts to foist Bathsheba's pregnancy off on Uriah. Deception in the realization of divine purpose (propagation of the people) is not judged harshly; in contrast, David's deception (and subsequent murder) of Uriah is condemned and punished.

Two of the three ancestresses/mothers of kings take an exterior memento of the occasion. Tamar takes Judah's staff and signet (Gen. 38:17-18), and Ruth takes an apron full of grain home to Naomi (Ruth 3:15). Bathsheba takes only the seed in her body away from the encounter. She does not defend her actions (by identifying the accuser as the perpetrator) as Tamar does, and she is not responsible as a daughter (like Ruth). Bathsheba acts as an independent agent and has no memento except what she sought: conception.

Interestingly, each of these unusual alliances involves a third party in the behind-the-scenes arrangements. Judah seeks to redeem his pledge by sending the promised kid with his friend the

Adullamite (Gen 38:20) Ruth is sent to the threshing floor by Naomi (Ruth 3:1-5); and Bathsheba is identified by "someone" and brought to the king by "messengers" (2 Sam 11:3). Actions, casual or not, may become significant as events unfold, and they are witnessed.

The goal of each of the ancestresses/mothers of kings is presumed to include conception. Tamar certainly wishes to conceive in the line of Judah. Ruth, widowed without children, obeys Naomi's wish that she marry, with conception implicit; and Bathsheba, childless, may be presumed to desire conception. Furthermore, two of these three women conceive from a single sexual encounter. Tamar conceives twins by Judah, and Bathsheba bears a son.[29] Ruth's conception is not attributed to her meeting with Boaz on the threshing floor, but the text suggests that she conceives without any delay (Ruth 4:13). These narratives portray ancestresses of kings as highly fertile.

Intertextual reading suggests that both Tamar's and Ruth's initiation of the sexual act subtly reinforces Bathsheba's active role in her sexual encounter with David. Furthermore, like her forebears as mothers of royal lineage, Bathsheba is determined to fulfill her role as a woman, even by unorthodox means.

The repeated motif of female initiative in female progenitors of kings suggests this is an acceptable quality in a woman who is determined to bear children—sons, of course, in this male-dominated perspective. Significantly, these women are beautiful. James Williams observes that "The arche-mother's beauty is a code communicating that she is blessed and that her progeny will be favored. This seems to work out almost without exception for biblical persons."[30] They are also not driven by lust. Thus ancestresses/mothers of kings are both desirable to their husbands (beautiful) and safe as wives (not likely to be unfaithful). These narrative patterns suggest type-actions associated with mothers of kings, depicted in table 2.

Unlike these female royal precursors, earlier women—Sarah and Rachel, for example—turn to other women's fertility to supplant their own when they do not conceive. They doubt their fertility. In contrast, Tamar, Ruth and Bathsheba act as if they *know* they are capable of conception, and they find some means to realize their potential as woman, as mother. The story of Hannah, in 1 Sam 1:1, provides an interesting intermediary link. As in earlier narratives,

	Tamar	Ruth	Bathsheba
Motif			
Narrative quite sexual	X	X	X
Woman makes herself object of male desire	X	X	X
Encounter involves deception	X	X	X
Third party privy to encounter	X	X	X
Woman takes memento of occasion	X	X	0
Woman's goal is or may be conception	X	X	X
Woman conceives from single encounter	X	?	X
Child in direct line to future king	X	X	X
Woman's narrative ends with birth of son(s)	X	X	0

Table 2: Bathsheba—Female Progenitor of a King

another woman bears her husband's children, but not at Hannah's suggestion. Like the mothers of royal lineage, Hannah insists on her own conception; however, her conception takes place in response to prayer and is thus precipitated by God, not by her own initiative.

The ancestresses/mothers of kings, like other narrative women, are depicted as having one social function: breeding. However, these women know what they want and they take steps to get their desires by all means. Where legitimacy is equivocal, they purify themselves (Bathsheba), receive blessings (Ruth), or prove their rights (Tamar).[31] There is one dramatic difference between the Tamar/Ruth and Bathsheba narratives. The stories of the earlier women end with the birth of their sons, but Bathsheba continues to play an active role in the narrative; in fact, the narrative develops her individuality and strength as a king's mother. Alice Bach, comparing David's wives, observes: "Only Bathsheba, the wife of sexual intimacy, participates in the ongoing story of David's reign. The length of female textual life seems to be directly connected to the extent of sexual pleasure she provides her male creators."[32]

Bathsheba is not mentioned in the sickness and death of the son of adultery, though David's response is narrated in detail (2 Sam 12:15-23). After the infant's death, however, David "comforts" his wife Bathsheba, implying his recognition of her grief even as he validates her concern with motherhood. Bathsheba's second conception is thus not initiated merely by lust but, perhaps, by both compassion and sexual desire. Implicitly, the offspring of compassion and desire is more suitable to becoming a king than the product of casual carnal lust.

Bathsheba and Nathan

When King David is old, his political frailty is depicted through sexual impotence (1 Kgs 1:1-4).[33] Even a beautiful young maiden cannot warm him; she nurses him but "the king knew her not," and Abishag the Shunammite remains a virgin.[34] The political implications are immediately apparent as Adonijah seeks to usurp the throne. The frailty of David is also implicitly contrasted with the continuing vitality of Bathsheba and all the other characters presented.

It is Nathan, initially vehemently opposed to David's conduct in the Bathsheba affair,[35] who advises Bathsheba of Adonijah's actions to secure the kingship and how she must act to save her life and that of her son Solomon.[36] Nathan tells Bathsheba exactly what to say to the king: essentially, Bathsheba is to remind David of his vow that Solomon shall reign after him. Nathan promises he will come in after her and confirm her words. This scene is striking not only because of Nathan's sudden concord with Bathsheba, but also because this cooperation sounds like a conspiracy. Nathan's promise to confirm Bathsheba's words instills the idea that her words *need* verification: that they may not be true, that there possibly was no earlier vow. According to this reading, Nathan and Bathsheba are joining forces to ensure that Bathsheba's son becomes king, despite Adonijah's legitimate claim to succession as the elder son.

As charged by Nathan, Bathsheba goes to the king's chamber—which presumes some special standing and suggests Nathan's awareness of her privileges in choosing to approach David through her. With Bathsheba's appearance before David, the reader is once more reminded of the king's age and frailty; he is apparently limited to bed to conduct even political matters. Bathsheba finds "Abishag the Shunammite ministering to the king" but ignores the maiden: "She bowed and did obeisance to the king" (1 Kgs 1:15). The mention of Abishag's presence and Bathsheba's inattention to her suggests some tension between the women and could imply Bathsheba's resentment of the younger woman. In any case, this wordless encounter effectively reverses the secondary-woman role of earlier narratives: instead of being the mother of children while the primary wife is barren, this secondary woman cannot even arouse the husband to intercourse, let alone become pregnant. Bathsheba's aloofness also suggests her self-assurance and command of the situation. In contrast, David's weakness is reinforced by his brief, two-word reply to Bathsheba's homage.

She responds with a surprisingly vigorous speech. Bathsheba has seemed passive as she follows Nathan's counsel without a word in response to his directive, but her speech to David reveals her as assertive, expressing Nathan's ideas but with much more vigor than he suggests. (In the following citations, roman type identifies Bathsheba's verbatim repetition of Nathan's words, italics identify her additions and her change of verb tenses.)

Nathan's version:

> Did you not, O lord king, swear to your maidservant: "Your son Solomon shall succeed me as king, and he shall sit upon my throne? Why then has Adonijah become king?" (1 Kgs 1:13, JPS)

Bathsheba's version:

> "My lord, you yourself swore to your maidservant *by the Lord your God:* Your son Solomon shall succeed me as king, and he shall sit upon my throne." *Yet now* Adonijah has become king, *and you, my lord the king, know nothing about it. He has prepared a sacrificial feast of a great many oxen, fatlings, and sheep, and he has invited all the king's sons and Abiathar the priest, and Joab commander of the army; but he has not invited your servant Solomon. And so the eyes of all Israel are upon you, O lord king, to tell them who shall succeed my lord*

the king on the throne. Otherwise, when my lord the king lies down
with his father, my son Solomon and I will be regarded as traitors' (1
Kgs 1:17-21, JPS)

Fokkelman notes that the essential information is contained in
Nathan's version, which Bathsheba converts from his recom-
mended humble questions into a much stronger, assertive declara-
tion.[37] With her direct remark, "You know nothing about"
Adonijah's making himself king, Bathsheba "dares to confront
David squarely with his impotence."[38] These are not the words of a
submissive, docile woman. Either Bathsheba has undergone a complete change of personality since David seduced her, or she then, as
now, is as much in control of her fate as she could be in a patriarchal
society. Her setting David up for seduction, according to this reading, is no more shocking than her using YHWH's name to "reinforce"
a vow that most likely had not taken place—but is validated by a
subsequent vow. Bathsheba is revealed as a resourceful, determined
woman who struggles within the system—with any means at
hand—to achieve her goals.

As prearranged, Nathan enters and corroborates Bathsheba's
words, using phrases closer to those of Bathsheba than the ones he
had originally proposed for her.

Nathan's new version:

O lord king, you must have said, "Adonijah shall succeed me as king,
and he shall sit upon my throne." For he has gone down today, and
has prepared a sacrificial feast of a great many oxen, fatlings, and
sheep. He invited all the king's sons and the army officers *and Abi-*
athar the priest. At this very moment they are eating and drinking
with him, and they are shouting, "Long live King Adonijah!" But he
did not invite me, your servant, or the priest Zadok, or Benaiah the
son of Jehoida, or *your servant Solomon.* Can this decision have
come from my lord the king, without your telling your servant *who*
is to succeed to the throne of my lord the king? (1 Kgs 1:23-27, JPS)

The implication is that Nathan has listened, and his adoption of
Bathsheba's words recognizes not only the merit of Bathsheba's
presentation but also the force of her personality. We must keep in

mind that this is a high-ranking male prophet using—following—the words of a woman. Nathan and Bathsheba are cooperating, using or leaving out each other's words, adding their own touches, to their mutual advantage.

The scene ends with David calling Bathsheba back into his presence. This time, Bathsheba does not bow upon her entrance; she stands and awaits David's response to her appeal and Nathan's. David then swears an oath, using the very words Bathsheba had used to describe his earlier oath (1 Kgs 1:13de = 1:17cd), claimed by Bathsheba and Nathan, as the core of the new and validating vow. Bathsheba's evocation of "by YHWH *your* God" (1:17)—which hedges her involvement with the alleged earlier oath—is changed to a larger perspective by David: "I have sworn by YHWH, the God of Israel" (1:30).

With David's oath to make Solomon his successor, "this very day" (1:30), Bathsheba does prostrate herself before him, "with her face to the ground, does obeisance to the king, and says, 'May my lord King David live forever!'" (1:31). David, she implies, will live on in her son Solomon. Bathsheba and Nathan have accomplished their goal: Solomon becomes king, Nathan remains a court prophet and Bathsheba remains in a position of power, shifting from king's wife to king's mother.

Bathsheba, King's Mother

No sooner is David buried than Adonijah comes to ask Bathsheba, now mother of the king, to act as intermediary to Solomon in Adonijah's desire to have Abishag the Shunammite—formerly ministering to David—as wife. Bathsheba is initially cautious, asking, "Do you come peaceably?" (1 Kgs. 2:13). Assuring her that he does come peaceably, Adonijah shows Bathsheba the respect due the king's mother by asking permission to speak: "I have something to say to you" (2:14), and she grants him that permission. Adonijah initially acknowledges the political situation: the kingship was his and has "become his brother's, for it was his from the Lord" (2:15), thus accepting the loss of kingship. However, he still has one request to make of Bathsheba, and she once more grants him permission to speak. Observing the close relationship between mother-queen and son-king, Adonijah believes "he [Solomon] will not refuse you" (2:17). Adonijah desires that Bathsheba act as negotiator between himself and Solomon to get Abishag the Shunammite as wife.

This sequence demonstrates the deference and honor accorded the king's mother both from the court and from her son ("he will not refuse you"). King Solomon does honor his mother's appearance, rising to meet her and bowing down to her, sitting on his throne but commanding a seat be brought "for the king's mother; and she sat on his right" (2:19). Bathsheba asks for "one small request," and "do not refuse me" (2:20). Solomon graciously acquiesces, "Make your request, my mother; for I will not refuse you" (2:20). However, when Bathsheba asks that Abishag the Shunammite be given his brother Adonijah as wife, King Solomon immediately repudiates his promise to his mother:

> "And why do you ask Abishag the Shunammite for Adonijah? Ask for him the kingdom also; for he is my elder brother, and on his side are Abiathar the priest and Joab the son of Zeruiah." Then King Solomon swore by the Lord, saying, "God do so to me and more also if this word does not cost Adonijah his life! Now therefore as the Lord lives, who has established me, and who has made me a house, as he promised, Adonijah shall be put to death this day." (1 Kgs 2:22-24, jps).

Although the text says that David never "knew" her, Abishag does belong to the king's concubines, and is therefore symbolic of the king's sexual/political power. Whoever sleeps with the king's women is, implicitly, king; for example, in the political intrigue over David's heir to the throne, Solomon's brother Absalom challenged David's kingship by sleeping with David's concubines. He took this action on the advice of Ahitophel, whose counsel was esteemed and surely reflected the custom of the people (2 Sam 16:20-23). In this context, where sexual prowess is clearly equated with political prowess, this is a precarious move by Adonijah. Significantly, in his appeal to Bathsheba, Adonijah minimizes his claim to political power by *asking* Solomon for Abishag, instead of taking her. He does not threaten Solomon, though the throne is his by right of primogeniture. But Bathsheba does not convey these mitigating aspects to Solomon. It is difficult to imagine this resourceful woman to be so dull with regard to court etiquette and intrigues that she presents Adonijah's case naively. I suggest that, although she asks Solomon not to refuse her, her presentation of Adonijah's case assures that Solomon *will refuse*, thus eliminating a potential rival for the throne and a potential danger to her and her son's position.

Bathsheba completes the paradigm established by Ruth and Tamar, and she develops that paradigm in a way impossible to the earlier ancestresses of kings. Reading Bathsheba in this light renders her wholly consistent in the two phases of her life recorded in the text: as conceiving woman and as protecting/guiding mother. Motherhood—conception and its continuation as nurturing/protecting—is presented as the dominating force for a woman. Sexual drive is ascribed to males: David desires Bathsheba and takes her, but sexual drive is denied esteemed future mothers of patriarchs and kings in the Davidic line.

Bathsheba's deceptive "appeal" to Solomon is her last appearance. There is no mention of her death in the text. Once she has contributed to Solomon's being securely established on the throne (1 Kings 2), her mothering role seems to be complete—and she is secure in her position as king's mother. Similarly, Tamar and Ruth disappear from the text when their roles as mother have been fulfilled. The ancestresses were resourceful bearers of sons in the royal lineage, but their stories relate no further roles in their sons' lives. In this reading, Bathsheba—like her predecessors—takes an enterprising role in conception and continues to take a dynamic role in her son's struggle for power. She extends the protecting and guiding of motherhood into her son's manhood; but when the possibility of mothering no longer exists—when her son is secure in the kingship—she too disappears from the text.

Bathsheba is neither temptress nor victim—and she is both. Her story is the tale of a woman determined to become as fully functioning a member of her society as is possible for a woman. This goal requires that she become a mother, and her story reflects her resourcefulness in achieving this. Hers is the story of sought-after conceptions, including that of a future king; maternal actions for protecting her son and securing his reign as king; actions as a king's mother to ensure the continued reign of her son-king, and vanishing with the cessation of that role. These are the milestones and vanishing point in the life of the woman who becomes the first narrated mother of a king and a textual paradigm for mothers of kings—and, by extension, for women who want to live full lives within gendered social constraints.

Job and the Womb

*J*ob's consistent protest is that he is unjustly punished, that he is righteous. All the male disputants also consider him righteous, although his friends insist he must have sinned, albeit unknowingly, to be suffering. Job defends his own righteousness and challenges God to prove him deserving of his punishment. God, instead, shows Job how little he knows of God's powers. He rewards Job and leaves the reader thinking that Job is, indeed, righteous.

By whose standards? Divine? Human, male and female, or only male? Job's wife, the only female to have voice in the book, agrees that her husband "maintains his integrity," but integrity is not necessarily righteousness. "Integrity" refers to unimpaired adherence to a code of values, whereas "righteousness" involves acting in accord with divine or moral law.[1] Are Job's integrity and righteousness in accord with one another? Does his righteousness have one import when applied to males and another when applied to females?

In order to ask these questions of the text, I direct my inquiry to the *form* of the text to search out what is ideologically significant in inconsistencies, gaps, unexpected elements or surprises; and to the *use of language*, such as symbolization, abstractions and displacement, in order to confront the way meaning is produced. By so doing, this paper seeks to explore what Hayden White calls the "misrepresentations of reality" implicit in the text of Job.[2]

In a book structured on debate, any deviation in presentation, style, technique or length may result in a significant discrepancy of form. We note that Job's wife has two lines of speech in the opening frame narrative (and the new daughters are singled out for mention in the closing narrative); otherwise the presence of females is ambiguous. They are either present and silent, or else absent: and no female voice is heard throughout the entire central poetic section. Either way, women do not talk but are talked about. Although the book addresses subject matter applicable to all humanity, females as well as males, the form of the book is inconsistent with reality in that women are entirely excluded from the central, poetic portion. This exclusion of women suggests an avenue of exploration.[3] If valid, this disparity will be repeated in other deviations of form and in the use of language, generating misrepresentations offered as reality.

Other disparities of form become apparent when the speeches of the several male discussants are compared with that of the one female. Job's wife has very few words—six in all. Women tend to have fewer words than men in the Hebrew Bible, which is not surprising given the patriarchal orientation of the book, but the disparity is extreme in Job, especially when compared to the verbosity of the male debaters.[4]

Another difference is in the style of the speeches: the words of Job's wife are not metaphoric, as those of the men are; and, in diametric and deleterious contrast, she implies cursing of God whereas they praise him. Furthermore, the woman uses none of the formalities of dispute observed by the male speakers. The disputes between Job and his friends observe a regular structure. N.H. Tur-Sinai has commented on the purposefulness and precision of detail.

> Every speech opened with some introductory verses, in which the orator asked for permission to speak. He then quoted an utterance of his opponent which was to be the subject of counter arguments. After refuting his opponent, and after a sentence or two bespeaking the attention of the latter, he stated his own view and tried to prove it. He wound up on a comforting or forbidding note designed, as it were, to preclude any further argument.... Each point in this debate fabric was supported by evidence.[5]

The substance of the male debates proffers arguments and proofs drawn from folk wisdom and the natural sciences of native and foreign peoples to support the testimony of facts or authority offered by the debating men. In contrast, Job's wife speaks without formal structure and without demonstrating the logic of her reasoning. Her words in 2:9 permit the reader to infer a syllogism:

If   You live to bless God
And   Your life is worse than death
Then Curse (bless) God and die.[6]

Logical reasoning is implied, not stated. Although the wife may be offering the logical conclusion of her deliberations, Job's chastising response conveys his presumption that her words are not thought out but spontaneous. Job's wife is the only character in the entire book who speaks without verbalizing a process of reasoning.

Rhetorically, the woman's initial words look like either praising or else chiding: "You still clutching your integrity?" (2:9). We may note that although rhetorical questions constitute a paramount literary device, used by all of the speakers, Job's wife is the only speaker in the book who uses rhetorical questions preponderantly. From the Adversary to Job and his friends to God, these questions, frequently in a series, serve to open an argument or to focus an argument that has already been developed. While the three friends illustrate approaches to rationality and Elihu offers a youthful but worthwhile argument, God offers the ultimate argument, and his argument is exclusively rhetorical. Job and his friends' rhetorical questions are freely argued and answered. In contrast, God's rhetorical questions seem to be understood as beyond challenge, and those of the wife as beneath competence. Both God and the wife remain unanswered. The wife, with a single question, challenges her husband strictly rhetorically, providing her own answer and thereby exempting Job from the necessity of an answer.[7] The textual use of rhetoric differentiates the female speaker from the male human (to distinguish from the divine) speakers, and contrasts the female ironically with God.

A further aspect in which the speech of Job's wife deviates from all other speeches is in its use of language. The beauty of the male disputes is in the play of figurative language far more than in the structural formality or sophistication of reasoning. But Job's wife is afforded no dramatic images, no grandiose metaphors. The males in the book express their opinions and their desires in the formality of dispute, the fashion of reasoning and the art of language, whereas female opinion and desire are exposed with neither formal or logical containment nor beauty of language: on all three counts, the wife's speech is differentiated from all others in the book. Woman is almost silenced, is relegated to the periphery, is afforded none of the customs valued by males, and is given words that no human male utters ("Curse God," 2:9). It seems that the curse uttered by his wife prompts Job to equate her with the "wicked": "You speak as one of the wicked [women] would speak indeed" (2:10); but as we shall see, an analysis of the language reveals that more is involved.[8]

Related to the namelessness of Job's wife is the fact that her words are relegated to the narrative frame story, which provides a background for the all-male enclave in the poetic center of the book. As Job's wife appears in the opening prose section of the frame story, the "replacement" daughters are given unusual emphasis in the closing section. The children who were so callously eliminated in the prologue (chs. 1–2) are replaced in the epilogue (42:13-15), but there is no further mention of the wife. Her role in child bearing is subsumed though she has presumably borne twenty children. In what might look like an alleviation of this misogyny, the daughters in the closing narrative section are specifically named even though the sons are not. They are "dove" (*Yemimah*)[9] "fragrance" (*Keṣi'ah*)[10] and "horn of eye shadow" (*Qeren-hapûk*).[11] The daughters are further described as beautiful: "In all the land there were no women so fair as Job's daughters" (42:15). Two of the three names allude to qualities that men desire in woman: sweet fragrance and the seductive charm associated with cosmetics and beauty; and we may infer that the third, "dove,"[12] had a similar connotation possibly associated with its soft, cooing sound.[13]

These daughters are capable of creating desire in men and are valued for it: Job gives them inheritance among their brothers (42:15). Ilana Pardes interprets this generosity as proof of the book's new-found understanding of women,[14] but such understanding does not accord with the fact that Job's wife still has no name and has, in fact, disappeared. In contrast, I suggest, the text discloses that masculine desire is experienced as pleasurable when its object is beautiful, desirable and unattainable maidens/daughters; but masculine desire per se is otherwise feared and denigrated, and it is foisted off on mature, accessible women. The latent misogyny is reasserted when Job is described as living to an old age to see his sons' sons to four generations. Daughters, despite their inheritances, do not carry the father's name; their descendants are apparently of little interest to Job. Naming females or not suggests that mature women, mothers, are in a different realm from young, nubile daughters in this text. We will return to this issue presently.

The "wickedness" of women is underscored by Job's wife being the only speaker in the book who remains nameless, another deviation of form. Biblical literature repeatedly demonstrates that failing to have a name and to pass on one's name is tantamount to not existing. The significance of names, of patrimony, even of territory, is so pervasive that naming can be used ironically, as in the Samson narrative.[15] Clearly, there is no irony in the namelessness of Job's wife. Indeed, after her words, she vanishes in and from the text even though she implicitly bears a second round of ten children.

Finally, only Job's wife is identified with the Adversary. Moshe Greenberg has pointed out the irony in the wife's "expressing her exasperation with her husband in the very terms used by God to praise him ("still hold on to your integrity?")," and in her "unwittingly [advocating] the Adversary's cause to Job."[16] It is not accidental that a woman's mouth, however innocently, echoes the Adversary's words. This subtle but unambiguous association of the Adversary and Job's wife—evil and woman, both personified—is consistent with and reinforces the derogatory subtext about woman that is conveyed in anomalies of form in an otherwise homogeneous text.[17] These textual incongruities consistently segregate Job's wife, paradigm of woman, from the male world; but they fail to provide much understanding beyond a discernible misogyny. Let us turn to language analysis to see if the differences in form are reflected in the use of language and to explore what, if anything, is revealed thereby.

The text offers an opening in that it is singularly focused on what Job wants: to be recognized as "righteous" despite his suffering. Job's desire is clear, but what does the text show that his wife desires?[18] Although Job's wife does not use a word for desire, her words make clear that her desire is directed only toward her husband; there is no suggestion of her own suffering. The distress conveyed in her words is the burden she emphatically feels for her husband's suffering. Her desire is that his agony be ended, whatever the cost, when his life is worse than death: "Curse God and die!"

As his wife never thinks of herself, Job never thinks of her. He thinks of his friends as he poses retorts to their presumptions of guilt, and he thinks of God as he demands a response to his questions; but these thoughts all ultimately turn on himself. Job professes to desire the goodness that God wishes of his people, but Job's goodness is without compassion; it is "ritually correct." He has offered burnt sacrifices to counter any hidden, forbidden thoughts his children may have had (1:5), with the implication that he is protecting *his* extended household. Even Job's expansive protests (29:7-25) celebrate his self-righteous social pleasure in his integrity. It is apparent that Job's primary desire is not only to *be* just but also to be *recognized* as just; recognition is proof of his position. Inasmuch as the text does not fault Job for his self-centeredness, this quality is apparently not to be condemned in a man; it suggests that males are socially experienced as egocentric. We note that woman's desire is not directed toward herself (or even her children) but is also focused on the male's needs. By the same token of social perceptions, the text assumes that woman is expected to deny herself and concentrate totally on her husband.

In the dialogue between Job and his friends, a range of terms for desire (not always exact synonyms) is used.[19] Despite the prominence of words for desire, only once does Job say specifically what it is he desires:

> I *desire* (*'ehpāṣ*) to speak to the Almighty and to argue with
> God . . . (13:3)

Nevertheless, expressions of desire permeate the debates (the speaker's name precedes each quotation):

Eliphaz: Is not your fear of God your confidence, your *hope*
(*tiqwāt*^e*kah*) the integrity of your ways? (4:6)

Eliphaz: the thirsty [ones] *pant with desire* (*šā'āph*) after his
wealth (5:5)

Job: Like a slave *longing* (*yiš'aph*) . . . (7:2)

Bildad: So the *hope of* (*tiqwath*) the ungodly shall perish (8:13)

Job: Though he *wished* (*yaḥpoṣ*) to dispute with him (9:3)

Job: You will *long for* (*tiksoph*) the work of your hands (14:15)

Job: Where then is *my hope* (*tiqwāthî*) and who shall see *my
hope* (*tiqwāthî*) (17:15)

Zophar: surely he will not know respite from *his cravings*
(*b*^e*biṭnô*); his *desired* things (*ḥamûdô*) will not save him
(20:20)

Zophar: When he has filled *his belly* (*biṭnô*, his seat of desire), he
will vent his anger (20:23)

Job: We have no *desire* (*ḥāphāṣ*^e*nû*) to know your ways (21:14)

Job: what does he *desire* (*ḥephṣô*) for the family he leaves behind? (21:21)

Job: He [God] does what his being *desires* (*'iwwtāh*) (23:13)

Job: What is the *hope of* (*tiqwath*) the ungodly? (27:8)

Job: If my heart has been *enticed* (*niphtāh*) by a woman (31:9)

Job: If I have kept the poor from their *desire* (*hepheṣ*) (31:16)

Job: If my heart was secretly *enticed* (*wayyipheth*) (31:27)

Elihu: I *desire* (*ḥāphaṣtî*) to clear you (33:32)

Elihu: I *entreat* (*'ābî*) that Job be tried (34:36)

Elihu: Do not *desire* (*tiš'aph*) the night to clear you (36:20)

God: Will he *wish* (*h*^a*yo'beh*), the wild ox, to serve you? (39:9)

Aside from Job's one statement of desire (13:3)—to argue with
God, which is normally beyond realization—Job and his friends attribute desire to others: the poor, the envious, the slave, or God;
otherwise, desire is expressed in the negative or subjunctive. These
are all "safe" desires: presumably beyond fulfillment, ascribed to
others, or denied and thus distanced—despite their being passionately expressed. Significantly, words for desire of a woman are used
only in denial. Job disclaims that he has looked at a maiden (31:1),

using a euphemism even to make that statement, and never alludes
to desiring a woman, including his wife.

> I have made a covenant with my eyes, so how can I *look* (*'ethbônēn,*
> Hithpael) at a virgin (31:1)

The word "look," which implies "desire," is usually interpreted as
"look lustfully" (NIV) or "look intently" (KJV), but the root of this
word (*byn*) implies "understanding," "discernment," and in the
Hithpael "show oneself attentive, consider diligently."[20] Such language intellectualizes and abstracts the danger of desire, thus dis-
tancing desire even as it is verbalized. No word for lust is put into
Job's mouth, even in repudiation. Job further emphasizes his dis-
tancing from desire: when he denies that his heart has been enticed
by another woman, he evokes a punishment that is sexual and explicit, but is inflicted on his wife, not himself: his wife would "grind
for another man and let others crouch over her" (31:10). The grind-
ing, presumably of grain, also has a sexual innuendo, as Athalya
Brenner has shown by calling attention to "the image of two mill-
stones, one on top of the other."[21] If Job has sinned, he says, let his
wife satisfy another man's needs. Even if he knows the punishment
is irrelevant because he has not sinned, Job invokes sin and servi-
tude for his wife as appropriate compensation for his own hypothetical sins. He also defines the wife's role: to prepare food for and
submit to her husband sexually. Desire is not acknowledged in either partner, which connotes a strong element of repression; and no
mention is made of the wife's function as mother (but see below).
This brings us back to the matter of mature women and motherhood—once again postponed.

The closest Job comes to acknowledging his own sexuality is his
complaint that his wife finds him repulsive because of his breath:

> My sigh is strange, loathsome (*zārāh*) to my wife (19:17)

The adjective used to describe Job's breath is derived from the verb
root *zwr*, "be loathsome," a cognate of the verb *ṣwr*, "be a stranger."[22]
Rendered in the feminine singular, but with the accent on the first
syllable, the adjective *zārāh* is visually identical with the adjective

associated with woman, *'iššāh zārāh,* a strange woman or harlot.[23] The choice of this adjective suggests that sexual implications are associated with Job's loathsome breath. Furthermore, comments by Tur-Sinai sustain the sexual innuendo. Differentiating *rûḥî,* "sigh," from *ruaḥ,* "wind, spirit," Tur-Sinai equates it with the parallel verb in the corresponding stich, Hebrew *ḥannōtî,* which he understands as "to sigh with desire."[24] Apparently Job, despite his sores and scabs, would be intimate with his wife, judging by the words he uses to couch her repudiation of him. However, no desire for his wife is verbalized. The text does not confound Job's desire for justice with more mundane desires, which are left ambiguous.

Even the desirability of woman is rendered dangerous. Job protests he could not "look upon a virgin" (31:1) and that his "heart has [not] been enticed by a woman" (31:9). Man's only defense against what is perceived as the "lure" of woman is to abstain from even looking, lest that lead to covetousness. It is thus woman, not man's desires, that generates this male anticovenantal behavior. Desire for woman is superseded by passion for God, expressed in dialogue between the men as they reason probable cause and effect relative to Job's condition. Whereas sexual desire is suppressed or denied, reason is valued by the men; and the book celebrates the logical give-and-take of disputations between Job and his friends, and between God and the Adversary. There is no suggestion that Job and his friends are not passionate in their disputes, but their eloquent expressions of desire are controlled by formality and logic, not subject to the illogic of emotional desire.

The male voices may seek to control, repress, deny the other half of humanity, but they cannot. Although woman has no voice in the central poetic chapters of the book, she is not forgotten; ironically, the men keep talking about her in the poetry. Interestingly, it is not in her role as femme fatale that woman haunts the male voices. She may occasionally cause men pain through her seductive powers, but the men allude to her more frequently as being an agent of life's grief by *giving birth.* Woman is so identified with childbearing that she may vanish in the image: the womb frequently becomes a synecdoche for woman, with woman "disappearing" in the anatomical part. Job questions, "Why did I not die from the womb (*mēreḥem*), come forth from the womb (*mibbeṭen*) and expire?" (3:11).[25]

Exploration of "desire" has led, by way of suppression of females, to the womb, which is specifically referred to twelve times in the Book of Job. Curiously, two words, *beten* and *reḥem,* are used as synonymous designations for "womb," and are carefully balanced in the text. The words alternate so consistently that almost any time *beten* is mentioned, *reḥem* follows, and vice versa.[26]

1:21	*beten*				
3:10	*beten*	3:11	*reḥem*	3:11	*beten*
10:18	*reḥem*	10:19	*beten*		
19:17	*beten*				
24:20	*beten*				
31:15	*beten*	31:15	*reḥem*	31:18	*beten*
38:8	*reḥem*	38:29	*beten*		

Whereas *reḥem* refers specifically to the womb, *beten* pertains primarily to "belly" in the sense of "source of hunger" or "abdomen"; and it is also used in Job in this sense (15:2; 20:23; 32:18, 19; 40:16). However, Job uses *beten* more frequently in its secondary sense, to refer to the female organ of reproduction.[27]

Two verses that allude to "womb" specifically identify the woman with whom the womb is associated, and both times the woman is Job's mother:

> Naked I came from the *womb* (*beten*) of *my mother* . . . (1:21)
> from the *womb* (*beten*) of *my mother* I guided . . . (31:18)

A further ten references to "womb" use the word as a synecdoche for woman as the agent of birth:

> for he did not shut the doors of my *womb* (*beten*) (3:10)

> Why did I not perish from the *womb* (*reḥem*) and die as I came from the *womb* (*beten*)? (3:11)

> Why then did you bring me out of the *womb* (*reḥem*)? (10:18)

> straight from the *womb* (*beten*) to the grave! (10:19)

The *womb* (*rehem*) forgets them . . . (24:20)

Did not he who made me in the *womb* (*beten*) make him? And he formed us the same in the *womb* (*rehem*). (31:15)

In these verses, woman is reduced to a womb; but in three additional verses, the womb is claimed by male voices, however figuratively. Listen to Job:

I am loathsome to the sons of *my womb* (*bitnî*). (19:17)[28]

I suggest that Job alludes to his wife, his "womb," as his possession and thereby figuratively claims her womb as his. The sense of the verse suggests that his sons are repelled by him (though all his biological sons have died at the hands of the Adversary).[29]

God evokes a "cosmic" womb through figurative language.

Or [who] stopped up the sea with doors when it gushed forth from the *womb* (*rehem*)? (38:8)

In this verse, YHWH simultaneously claims a womb and images the womb as a source of death. The sea, the life force, threatens to overwhelm, bringing death, and must be contained by closing doors against death—and life. What results is, as Alter suggests, "a virtual oxymoron, expressing a paradoxical feeling that God's creation involves a necessary holding in check of destructive forces and a sustaining of those same forces because they are also forces of life."[30] In another verse, the implication is that God's womb delivers ice, also an image of life and death:

from whose *womb* (*beten*) comes the ice? (38.29)

Significantly, both life and death are identified with the woman's womb, decried by males but claimed by both earthly man and the male God.

The poetic chapters of Job reduce woman to a receptacle for birth and, thereby, the pain man—not woman—endures in life. "Man that is born of woman is of few days and full of trouble" (14:1) and "What is man, that he can be clean? Or he that is born of a woman, that he can be righteous?" (15:14). Even man's inability to achieve purity, accepted in these lines, is subsequently displaced upon woman: "How then can man be righteous before God? How can he who is born of woman be clean?" (25:4).

If a woman is not equated with a womb by virtue of childlessness, then she is an object of utmost pity, as expressed by redundant adjectives and invidious comparison: "the barren childless woman" is linked with "the abject widow" (24:21). Woman is either a womb that gives birth to man's grief or a failed womb. It is hard to know which is better. Either way, there is no potential for woman to be righteous in this text.

The Book of Job overtly weighs, in elaborately metaphorical language, the logical give-and-take of disputations between Job and his friends, and between God and the Adversary, to evaluate Job's claim to righteousness. Only desolate language, with merely tacit systematic reasoning, is attributed to Job's wife, woman personified— otherwise reduced to a womb.

Analysis of form and language discloses Job's proclaimed righteousness to be the posturing of a male—of a patriarchal society, including God—manifestly at the expense of woman. Paradoxically, Job *is* righteous—in accord with divine law, personified by God—in this text, despite the misogyny that contradicts the strictures of Torah, for instance, "Honor your father and mother" (Exod 20:12). However, the use of language by males is shown to incorporate a subtext of preoccupation with females, specifically female reproductive powers. This coupled rejection of woman and suppressed interest in woman's sexual functions discloses a significant fissure in the overt male concerns about righteousness depicted in Job.

6

Michal, the Barren Wife

*D*avid's procreativity is substantiated by the sons he fathers by each of his many wives[1]—with the singular exception of his wife Michal, who remains childless "to her dying day" (2 Sam 6:23). It seems clear that the infertility in this instance lies with the woman, with Michal,[2] but there still remains the significance of her infertility. In biblical texts women may be "forgotten" by God, as Sarah is (Gen 17:17),[3] or they may fail to conceive because God favors another woman's conception, as Rachel is barren while her sister Leah repeatedly bears sons (Gen 29:31). God usually remembers or rectifies his judgment, resulting in the woman's long-delayed and much-anticipated pregnancy (e.g., Gen 30:22). Michal, however, remains infertile to the end of her life. The singularity of Michal's marked identification as a childless woman invites the reader to explore the sources and ramifications of her infertility.[4]

David is still a young man, as yet unmarried, and, as he puts it, "a poor man of no consequence" (1 Sam 18:23) when Saul offers his daughter Michal to him as wife. In fact, Michal is the second daughter Saul offers to David as wife. The daughter first offered, Merab, was the older, and—for no obvious reason—was instead given to another man.

Michal, we recall, is "given" to David by Saul, much as an object is given, and with the intention not of gaining a son-in-law but of disposing of David as a threat. In fact, Saul plots that Michal will serve as a "snare" to put David in a vulnerable position against the

Philistines (1 Sam 18:21). In effect, Saul gives Michal in marriage to David with the plan that David will be killed, thereby preventing the marriage. And when David and Michal *do* marry, Saul's intention is to widow his daughter, to kill his daughter's husband, whom she loves. Michal is thus caught in a triangle with her father and her husband, with Saul persecuting David out of jealousy. Saul's relationship to Michal is clearly less important to him than his jealousy of David. These messages from father to daughter do not show love or esteem, and they surely impinge upon Michal's perception of herself.

Furthermore, Michal is not described as "beautiful" like two of David's other significant wives, Abigail and Bathsheba. Indeed, David is nowhere described as even being attracted to Michal. The text suggests he marries her for his advantage. "David was pleased with becoming the king's son-in-law" (1 Sam 18:26). On the other hand, Michal is twice reported as loving David (1 Sam 18:20, 28).[5] Michal's position is not difficult to infer. She has not received love and validation from her father, and she is entering a similarly non-loving relationship with David.

Outwardly, Michal is in a privileged position. In a marriage in which Michal loves her husband but David presumably fulfills his conjugal duties, Michal may well confuse her social worth and prestige with love. It is conceivable that Michal's sense of her own worth is partially based on her position as daughter of the king; she could well have convinced herself that this handsome shepherd/warrior is actually enamored of her.

Inwardly—daughter as object, daughter less important to her father than revenge on a perceived enemy, daughter whose feelings are totally ignored—Michal is probably not emotionally secure. These circumstances may contribute to Michal's loving David, a man socially beneath her, as she seeks love and esteem from a man. Saul the king has not shown Michal love; perhaps she thinks David the shepherd/warrior will show the king's daughter that love. Michal presumably does not know that David's pleasure is in being the king's son-in-law (1 Sam 18:26) and not in being Michal's husband.

Instead of receiving validation from her loved one, Michal has, it seems, married a man much like her father. There is no indication that David has any regard for Michal. Significantly, in a society that

regards woman's role as bearer of children, Michal has not conceived while married to David. All of these elements contribute to
emotional shame. Nevertheless, Michal's conflict of inward shame
and privileged life do not destroy her capacity to love. Her strength
of character is indicated in that she does *not* continue in the victim
role established with her father. Instead, Michal acts as rescuer of
David in the triangulation with Saul: when Saul plots to kill his son-
in-law, Michal assumes a rescuer role to save her victim husband—
even though he is a warrior. She does not consult; she directs the
action; David silently complies. Saul persecutes David; Michal res-
cues David, thereby persecuting Saul. These actions show ambiva-
lence in Michal's relationships with males.

When Michal protects David from her father's orders to his messengers to kill him, she "let him down from the window" (1 Sam
19:12), an effort that took rapid planning and possibly physical
strength. Michal further postpones pursuit of David by putting *ter-
raphim*, household idols, in bed in his place and even claiming that
he is sick and cannot appear to Saul's messengers (1 Sam 19:14).

Saul insists that David be brought before him, in his sickbed if
need be; when her ruse is exposed, Michal lies to her father to justify her actions (1 Sam 19:17). In this demonstration of her allegiance, Michal "chooses her husband over her father; this is an
ironic anticipation of David's later rebuke to her that it was 'the
Lord who chose me rather than your father'" (2 Sam 6:21).[6] On a
practical level, Michal's lie permits her to remain safe from her father's wrath and possibly an integral part of the king's family
(though as a married woman she belongs to her husband's family).[7]
She acts resourcefully and admirably on behalf of her husband, but
betrays her father—who has already betrayed her in his actions.

One way of interpreting this series of events is in terms of
Michal's self-sacrifice. One could also regard Michal's sending
David away as a tacit recognition that her love for David has not
been reciprocated. The household idols she places in her bed to de-
ceive the king's messengers may be seen as symbolic representations
of her husband's behavior in their relationship: images of wood or
clay or stone or metal, unresponsive to the love Michal brought to
the marriage. The reader knows David *is* capable of showing love.
He has been affectionate, even kissing the passive, docile Jonathan

(1 Sam 20:41); the "image" Michal puts in their bed suggests that David has been less than warm-blooded—more like something cold and inorganic—in his marriage bed. The idols in bed permit Michal-as-rescuer to gain more time for David, permit Michal-as-daughter to save herself, permit Michal-as-wife a retreat from denied intimacy. In this interpretation, Michal is not yet aware of David's refusal to commit himself; she is not yet admitting to herself the reality of his lack of interest in their marriage. She is sending away the man whom she still loves, protecting his life but not going with him.

It may be protested that Michal could not go with David, that she could not live the life of a highwayman's wife, but this assumes that David and Michal already know that he will live that life when he leaves the royal household. That assumption seems unlikely since David's departure is spontaneous—an immediate result of Michal's information about Saul's plans to have David killed that night.

Could David and Michal have gone to David's parents' home for safety? What other options were possible for a couple who wished to stay together? Abraham and Sarah travel great distances, as do other patriarchs and their wives. Although they are not escaping from their own hostile king, those couples do face other hostile forces, both within and outside their own families. It was not impossible for a woman to travel with her husband. But Michal tells David to save his life (1 Sam 19:11) and sends David off alone. As a married woman, she is no longer technically a member of her father's household. Why does she choose to remain without her husband? Michal may be choosing to remain with a "known" pain—her relationship with her father; she may be making a total sacrifice to save her husband; or at some (unconscious?) level, Michal may be acknowledging David's lack of interest in her.

Before Michal and David come into contact again, David has taken six additional wives and has fathered one son by each of them. Danna Nolan Fewell and David M. Gunn find that "David's policy is to dissipate all power but his own. He will not have one wife but several. And no wife will be first in his house."[8] Before Michal and David meet again, Saul gives his married daughter Michal to another man, "Palti, son of Laish, who was from Gallim" (1 Sam 25:44).[9] Inasmuch as this bit of information immediately follows the news of David's having taken two wives, the reader may infer that Saul considers it unlikely that the much-married David will still claim Michal as wife, or that Saul is expressing his hostility to David by "killing" him symbolically with Michal's enforced "widowhood." Once again Michal is the victim. No mention is made of Michal's love of David, of her reaction to this turn of events or of her relationship to Palti.

After the death of Saul, a war between the house of Saul and the house of David develops, with Saul's followers in fragmented opposition to the increasingly powerful David. One follower, Abner, offers to make a pact with David, proposing to bring "all Israel" to David's side as a rebuke of Saul's son Ish-bosheth (2 Sam 3:12). David's surprising response is to accept the pact with the singular demand of his "wife, Michal, for whom I paid one hundred foreskins" (3:14). As her father "gave" her to David and to Palti, once again Michal is transferred from male to male as an object.

To complicate matters, the reader learns that Michal's new husband Palti is deeply attached to her; although the text does not explicitly say so, it seems safe to assume that he loves her (3:12-16).[10] When Ish-bosheth and Abner take her from Palti to return her to her (first) husband, David, the focus is not on Michal but on Palti. The initiative Michal demonstrated when she sent David away is replaced by a passive Michal and a helpless husband who walks with her, weeping. In fact, Palti does not turn back from walking beside Michal until he is ordered to do so. Palti's devotion and helplessness provide a marked contrast to David, who has become decisive and aggressive since his wordless escape from Michal's window. The reader is pulled in two directions: by Palti's love for Michal and by recollections of Michal's love for David. The textual silence about Michal's feelings for Palti may encourage the reader to hope that the reunion with David will renew her love for him—or it may signal that Michal is as helpless as Palti and, possibly, even angry about being returned to the husband whom she remembers as unloving and "wooden" in bed. The text is further silent about Michal's fruitfulness in her marriage to Palti. This silence may suggest that Michal has been infertile—that the impotent household idol she put in bed in place of David has indeed become symbolic of her lack of fecundity.

When David is king, he acts to bring the ark of God to the City of David with great celebration, including sacrifices and dancing to the music of "wood instruments, lyres, harps, timbrels, sistrums, and cymbals" (2 Sam 6:5).[11] David himself, "girt [only?] with a linen ephod," "whirled with all his might" in dancing before the Lord (2 Sam 6:14). The festivity of the shouts and blasts of the horn accompanying the progress of the awesome ark is captured by the spectacle of the whirling, ecstatic king, a sight Michal catches from behind a window.

The contrast of this scene at the window with the earlier window scene is notable. In the earlier scene, Michal represents the royal family as daughter of Saul, and David is the powerless son-in-law. In the later scene, David *is* royalty—the king—and Michal is merely one of several wives. The window that provided David freedom and saved his life becomes a window that confines Michal, evidenced by the bitter tone of her words. The window "frames" each of these scenes, much as it "frames" David's earlier speechless passivity, and his later surge of uninhibited activity. The window also "frames" the sexual content of each of the scenes: the marital bed with its representations of a powerless David as he leaves the first window scene, vis-à-vis the uninhibited, barely covered David kicking up his legs and exposing his genitalia before the mixed-gender throng in the second window scene. The reader is invited to consider the developments in the lives of the protagonists through this literary "window."

In the conclusion of this passage (2 Sam 6:20-23), King David distributes food to "the entire multitude of Israel, man and woman alike," before the people leave for their homes (6:19). One can well imagine the elation the king is enjoying when he returns to his own household. It is Michal who comes out to greet David upon his return—not with tambourines to welcome the returning hero but with caustic words. "Didn't the king of Israel do himself honor today—exposing himself in the sight of the slave girls of his subjects, as one of the riffraff might expose himself!" (6:20). These words reveal an image of Michal entirely different from the one we encountered when Michal last spoke—the young woman resourcefully saving her husband's life even as she sends him away from her side. Interim events have apparently made Michal angry and sharp-tongued. Michal may regret her separation from Palti; she may feel that David is "beneath her," as demonstrated by his exhibitionist behavior; she may resent the fact that she, who enjoyed the prestige of being the king's daughter, is merely one of several wives of this boorish king—and childless to boot. Michal's angry words to David suggest that she is displacing the shame she experiences in her situation onto David. David's response seizes on Michal's claim to royal breeding, but the narrator's commentary turns from the past to focus on the future: the text makes explicit that Michal remains childless:

> "It was before the Lord who chose me instead of your father and all his family and appointed me ruler over the Lord's people Israel! I will dance before the Lord and dishonor myself even more, and be low in your[12] esteem; but among the slave girls that you speak of I will be honored." And to her dying day Michal daughter of Saul had no children. (6:21-23)

In his response, David defends himself passionately, indicating Michal's continuing importance to him at some level. His emotional retaliation reveals his own discomfort—shame? guilt?—through his emotional defensiveness.

Michal's voice is only heard in the initial and final phases of her life, so there is no possibility of determining precisely what effects the change from a loving and enthusiastic woman to a bitter harridan. It is clear that her father and her husband[13] have bandied her about like chattel, from "man" to "man." But Michal has matured. Saul is now dead, and Michal is no longer in denial about her relationship with David. Freed of her father's abuse, Michal finally owns her own power by confronting David, by becoming a person, not an object. She regains her voice, but she remains childless.

It may be that David recalled Michal as wife to ensure that no offspring of Saul would threaten his line of succession. The text does leave open the remote possibility that Michal herself refuses to give David children: notice of her childlessness immediately follows David's remarks with an opening conjunction, "and," thus avoiding attributing, but not denying, any relationship between David's repudiation of Michal and her childlessness.[14] It is more likely that the text punishes Michal for her haughty words, which seem to ensure that David will not visit her bed and that Michal's childlessness is her punishment for speaking out against YHWH's anointed. In this reading, it is David, not Michal's own barrenness, who renders her childless. Michal has apparently never been pregnant, but David's implied reaction obviates the possibility of Michal's being a "late bloomer" like Sarah, Rebekah, and Hannah.

Even if David would visit her bed, the fact is that Michal is not in control of her capacity to reproduce. J. Cheryl Exum has suggested that "Since it is YHWH who opens and closes the womb (Gen 20:18; 29:31; 30:2, 22; 1 Sam 1:5, 6; Isa 66:9), perhaps the deity bears responsibility."[15] I propose the text subtly places the source of Michal's barrenness on Michal herself, symbolized by her putting household idols in her bed.

The text indicates that as a young woman Michal had, and may have worshiped, idols. Her putting the idols in her bed to take the place of the fleeing David carries a wealth of meaning: a clever ruse to give David time to flee, a symbol of David's relationship to Michal, and an exposure of her failure to worship the one God of the Israelites. A household idol is, after all, an image of a foreign god. As Peter Miscall observes, "Worship of foreign gods is the main snare, *môqeš*, in the narrative in Genesis—2 Kings."[16]

Since it is God who determines women's capacity to bear children in biblical texts, who remembers barren women and allows them to become pregnant, it seems likely that God would not remember Michal. We recall that Rachel, whom God remembered after many years of infertility (Gen 30:22), was punished after she stole her father's household idols—and they were not her own. Furthermore, when Jacob demands that all the "foreign gods" in the camp be brought to him for burial and purification before proceeding to Bethel (Gen 35:2-4), it is assumed that Rachel also relinquishes the idols she brought with her. In this delicate balance of fertility and faith, Rachel bears another son but dies at his birth.

Michal, however, is never shown to relinquish the idols she had available to put in her bed. Furthermore, Michal's ridiculing of David's ecstatic abandon depicts her as more interested in the propriety of royal behavior than joy in the one God. Michal is a barren wife, I suggest, because she has been portrayed as barren of belief in the God of Israel, the God who could open her womb. Thus God can be included among the males who persecute Michal. As a later text compares the works of God with those of idols (Judg 10:13), this text suggests that if Michal puts idols in her bed, let the idols make her pregnant. Michal is childless because she is depicted not as a God-fearing woman but as a woman who values her household gods and her royal status, a woman who presumes to think and act for herself, flying in the face of tradition rather than demurely moderating her social position and personal capacities. She is a loving and nurturing woman and a victim of male egocentricity. The author(s) of this text presents a complex portrait of Michal, one that evokes sympathy even as it condemns.

The first retelling of these events (1 Chron 15:29) focuses on David rather than Michal, paraphrasing only 2 Sam 16:16. Without the additional information provided in the books of Samuel, this one verse uses Michal, daughter of Saul, to highlight David's greatness. Rabbinic literature, however, is not so dismissive. In her valuable article, "Michal in Hebrew Sources," Tamara Eskenazi finds that "the rabbis generally praise her and sympathize not only with her but also with her second husband Palti."[17] Eskenazi also offers modern midrashic responses to Michal—which may portray her as a heroine or as a victim—and recent scholarly responses.[18] "As a compassionate sister, as romantic heroine or as a tragic victim, Michal in Hebrew literature is more often praised than blamed."[19] But each of these views is partial and thereby diminishes Michal's story.

Even though this narrative sequence is full of irresolvable gaps, Michal deserves to be accorded the complexity of her portrayal in the books of Samuel. She is depicted as a woman who has the capacity for love and nurturing, as evidenced by her early exchange with David; and as a woman reduced to a life of pain and ultimate oblivion by power-hungry men and an omnipotent and unforgiving. God. The saving grace of the men in her life is that they did not have, and probably did not worship, idols, whereas Michal apparently did. Readers have long accepted the flawed male protagonists of the Hebrew Bible. Michal serves as a female counterweight, denied a significant role because her flaw involves denial of the God of Israel. The male-dominated religious culture and its authors sacrificed Michal's admirable qualities to Saul's and David's self-aggrandizing ones. The punishment accorded her is the most harsh and unjust the biblical writers could wreak: her story depicts a woman's degradation from love and joy into a life of pain and shame, and suffering the worst insult of all: the failure of the one purpose in life that biblical women could aspire to achieve, motherhood and descendants.

Michal is yet another imperfect human being in the Hebrew Bible. As such, she deserves more than glorification or victimization. She deserves the full complex difficulty of her story.

Honor and Shame
in the Book of Esther

Introduction

The Book of Esther is held to offer a paradigm for Jewish life in the diaspora, as stated by Sidnie Ann White.[1] But this is only part of the picture. As exiles, the Jews are in a "dependent" position, one associated with females, whereas autonomy and power are associated with males. These male and female "roles"—representing, respectively, honor and shame—not only permeate the text of Esther, but are also used pointedly to "shame" the culture in which the Israelites are exiled and, by comparison, to "honor" the Israelites. The Persians may not, historically, have responded to the same honor/shame codes as the Israelites, but the text suggests that they did, and the narrative ridicules the dominant culture, personified by the king, in terms of communal values or those of the minority culture. It does so through the agency of a woman, apparently because women are normally identified with shame.[2]

To support this claim of honor/shame as a definitive cultural value among the Israelites in the text of Esther, current cultural anthropological theories and sociological field studies are invoked, correlating similar social groups that demonstrate analogous features of economic life and economic constraints.[3] Unlike those studies, the focus here is not on equating two social groups—one ancient, one modern; instead, honor/shame in contemporary sociological fieldwork is invoked to illuminate an ancient text. Working "backwards," reading biblical texts through the paradigms of contemporary research, establishes an analogy. An analogy is not a mirror, however, and absolute consistency is not to be expected. Indeed, the deviations are provocative and rewarding.

Today, "honor" is a term describing an obviously desirable condition involving recognition of self-worth and respect from others. In ancient (and some more recent) cultures, however, the term is involved with more specific conditions; and the primary condition for achieving honor is autonomy. One of the principal determinants of honor is sexual autonomy, and in the sexual sphere, only men could be autonomous. Women are marked as sexual beings by public awareness of menses and pregnancy, while men bear no outward witness of sexual activity. Therefore, in such a social structure, only men can be fully autonomous and be worthy of honor. Other elements of masculine honor involve providing for and protecting the reflected honor of the family, social prominence, manly courage and virility. Males can demonstrate their sexuality, even aggressively, but they are ostensibly capable of having that sexuality under control, whereas women, who menstruate and become pregnant, are not.

Women are not utterly denied honor, but usually they can only achieve it through "shame." In this context, shame achieves a positive value akin to honor, albeit not so obviously honorific. According to Lyn M. Bechtel, shame "relates to failure or inadequacy to reach or live up to a socio-parental goal or ideal";[4] and since women cannot achieve the honor associated with autonomy, they take pride in contributing to their males' honor through preservation of feminine modesty, that is, "shame." Furthermore, "shame" is to be clearly distinguished from "guilt" and from "being shamed."[5] Feminine "shame" as a positive value is characterized by deference and submission to male authority, by docile and timorous behavior, by hiding nakedness, by sexual exclusiveness, and by modesty in attire and deportment. The absence of these qualities renders a woman "shameless" and dishonors her family—particularly her husband, who cannot "control" his wife—in the eyes of the community: "a shameless person is one who does not recognize social boundaries."[6] A husband who fails in his obligations is likewise "shamed." To protect his honor and social reputation from his wife's shameful behavior, a husband has socially recognized strategies: segregation of his women, insisting that they remain veiled in public, and restricting their social behavior to "women's spaces."

Female spaces and female things are centered around the family residence and "face toward the inside," and all things remaining within the home are identified with the female; those taken from the inside to the outside—the male "space"—are identified with the male. Places of contact between the genders are "male when males are present" or when females are "properly chaperoned."[7] Accordingly, women are excluded from male social assemblies.

In her chapter on "Modesty, Gender and Sexuality," Lila Abu-Lughod points out that feminine modesty associates denial of sexuality with morality: "the more [women] deny their sexuality, the more honorable they are." Significantly, "The woman [who is modest] does not allow herself to be seen by men [and] does not appear when guests or strangers visit her household."[8] A modest woman forbears eating and talking in the presence of men. By suppressing her sexuality in front of men, a woman shows deference to and dependence upon males, thus validating their honor and prestige in the community. In this way, shame allows women to partake vicariously of honor.

These social values—honor and shame—constitute a "basic pattern of affect, of what is symbolically meaningful" in societies where social approval of authoritative figures is characteristic of the patriarchal, segmentary structure.[9] These honor/shame codes are most effective in group-oriented societies, which tend to stratify social status, defining ranks of authority: king, elder, parent, husband, wife. Each class has a subordinate from whom it claims deference.[10] The individual or group that fails to uphold community honor is shamed by publicly exposing his, her or their failure to realize the internalized ideals of the society. The passive construction—"is shamed," "being shamed"—conveys the lack of autonomy involved.

In ancient Israel, being shamed functioned in a range of contexts: judicial, political (including both warfare and diplomacy) and social. Tellingly, captive warriors of all ranks were stripped and led off naked and bound. Such nakedness exposed the prisoners to the elements and also exposed their genitals to public view. "Walking

naked entailed double shame. . . . Part of the socialization process in
Israel involved an awareness that public nakedness was inappropriate and unacceptable behavior."[11] Exposure of the genitals depicted
people as powerless and susceptible, putting males in the position
of "shameless" women, robbing them of their self-respect and
pride, and demeaning them in the community.

The Palace Milieu

Because the cultural value of honor/shame is diffused through the
entire Book of Esther, the book will be treated as a unit, disregard-
ing recent studies in the structure of the narrative that are valuable
in another context. It is noted, however, that the exposition of the
book is a self-contained narrative unit that provides background
material for the rest of the book and, in so doing, establishes foil
characters and foil situations, including honor/shame, against
which the main action can be interpreted.[12] Significantly, the abuse
of honor/shame in the exposition presages later developments.
These developments do not necessarily polarize honor/shame in in-
flexible patterns; instead, elements of honor/shame shift and com-
bine, revealing all-too-human individuals and a sophisticated text.

The narrative takes place in the royal palace of Persia; Ahasuerus's name may have been a title: "chief of rulers."[13] Apparently
to assert his power, his autonomy, his honor, this "chief of rulers"
gives two banquets, distinguished by duration and by those who attend. The guests at the first banquet are the courtiers and nobles of
the far-flung kingdom. As part of the aristocracy, these guests com-
prise a "natural" group based on degree of honor or power; and the
festivities last 180 days—approximately six months. The second
banquet recognizes a more intimate "natural" group, the "family" of
the palace, without regard for hierarchy.[14] The king's honor is en-
hanced by the opulence of both banquets and by his apparent authority over both kinds of natural groups: the ruling class of the
far-flung hierarchy and the inclusive palace contingent.

The first insinuation that the king's autonomy is not consistent
with his title occurs when these very banquets, which suggest redis-
tributive banquets of tribal societies,[15] make no mention of food. In

fact, the honor sought in relating the costly accoutrements of the palace is subtly undermined by the excessively protracted banquets (1:6-7)—which fail to mention food—and by the emphasis on drink (1:7-8).[16] This innuendo of inconsistency is reinforced when the king invites his courtiers to drink as much as they want: Ahasuerus places no restrictions on their drinking and thereby relinquishes his authority over their consumption.[17] They are not invited to eat as much as they want, which does not lead to loss of control, but are legally *decreed* to drink as much as they want, even to become drunk:[18] "And the drinking was by law without restraint, for the king had ordered his palace officials to do as each [man] wished" (1:8). Ahasuerus legally relinquishes his autonomy over his guests in this sphere and invites all of them—great and small—to do the same: relinquish autonomy over themselves. Since autonomy is essential to honor, the king's action undermines himself and his people. Thus, from the outset, the Esther narrative subtly (and repeatedly) proclaims the power and honor of Ahasuerus and his kingdom—and immediately, insidiously, undermines it.[19]

The king's questionable autonomy is further demonstrated after Ahasuerus uses his authority to command seven eunuchs to bring his queen, Vashti, to appear before the assembled nonkin males.[20] Bickerman observes that "By custom, the wedded wives could be present at Persian dinners (Neh 2:6). But they left when the drinking bout was to begin. At this time, concubines and courtesans came in." Bickerman implicitly acknowledges the element of honor/shame: "By coming to the king's party, Vashti would lose face, she would degrade herself to the position of a concubine."[21] Losing face, we recall, is one of the major elements of the honor/shame system.

Actually, the king's command is contrary to the basic tenets of honor/shame, for he commands his wife to enter masculine space inappropriately, forbidden a woman who values her sense of shame; and his command specifies only that she wear her royal crown. Rabbinic commentary has interpreted that command to specify that she wear only her royal crown and appear naked, and gives her credit for refusing.[22] The degree of clothing accentuates a basic problem. Even fully clothed, Vashti is faced with a dilemma: whether to relinquish her claim to honor through abandoning her modesty and appearing in a forbidden masculine space, or through defying her husband's authority. She chooses the latter.

When Vashti acts autonomously and refuses, the king again does not manifest his royal control or leadership in his response; he asks for the judgment of his wise men. These men are described as knowing "the times" (1:13), and the text suggests that this is the king's customary response. This "customary" response reinforces the image of the king as one who does not exercise his autonomy or authority independently but seeks sage advice. Despite the expectations of autonomic honor, Ahasuerus's practice of consulting sages can be taken as an encouraging sign (that he is not a tyrant, that he is seeking wisdom)—until the judgment of these "sages" reflects negatively on the king. Indeed, elements of this negative view of the king have been noted in scholarly literature. For instance, David Clines says, "The satire is against the king, Persians, men," and he even acknowledges that the king has "lost face."[23]

The "wise men" advise the king to dismiss Queen Vashti because, if her behavior is tolerated, the other wives (especially the wives of these courtiers?) might behave in a similar way and refuse to defer to their husbands. The whole honor/shame edifice might tumble if women were to assert their own autonomy, even to protect their own shame. The king acquiesces: he "leads" by following his courtiers.

When the king's wrath against Vashti has subsided, it is the king's servants who, in effect, initiate the search for a replacement. The servants direct, "Seek beautiful young virgins for the king. And the king will appoint officers. . . . And the young woman who pleases the king shall rule instead of Vashti" (2:2-4).

Once again, the authority of the king is undermined by others' autonomous words, this time words of relatively insignificant members of the palace household, words that direct not only what shall *be done* (seek virgins) but also what the king shall *do* (choose officers). Most surprising is the statement that the chosen woman will "rule instead of Vashti." It may be that the reader is to assume that the queen will "rule" over the harem, but the ambiguity, especially in light of Esther's subsequent actions, is provocative. The text has already delineated a paradoxically nonautonomous king, and this verse prefigures an (equally paradoxical) autonomous queen. Consistent in his character, the king once more follows the lead of his followers.

The Beauty Contest

At this juncture, Mordecai is introduced with full genealogy and history to explain his presence in Susa and his relationship with his niece, Esther, all of which serves to present Mordecai as a man of honor. Mordecai, we note, does not direct Esther to enter the beauty contest and remains uninvolved in this un-Jewish behavior. Nevertheless, he does nothing to interfere with Esther's entering into a situation foreign to Jews or her potential loss of shame. On her part, Esther's participation is passive, as befits a modest woman and a Jew in a foreign culture: "Esther was also brought to the king's house" (2:8). The question remains how Jewish values can be assimilated to a beauty contest and the possibility of harem life. I suggest that this episode foreshadows other events of the narrative that tacitly posit and approve that the Persian (diaspora) Jews maintain a "low profile," by publicly assimilating to the practices of the host culture and, in this instance, by not refusing to give up their virgins to the king's command. The narrative suggests that group survival supersedes even a "basic pattern of affect" such as honor/shame. (The conclusion of the story affirms that the Jewish community and Jewish identity is to be maintained intact, presumably in the seclusion of the Jewish home and community.)

This bid to judge women by their physical appearance recalls the king's command to Vashti to appear before and be admired by his courtiers. We may ask what the difference is between Vashti's display of her beauty and Esther's (and the other virgins'). Rabbinic commentary notwithstanding, the maidens' clothing—or lack thereof—is unknown. To my knowledge, no one has questioned the exposure required in the beauty contest; and it seems likely that Mordecai accedes with Esther's entering into a situation in which her beauty of body as well as of face will be judged—probably as fully exposed as Vashti, or more so.[24] A basic difference is that Vashti is *one* woman confronted in *male space* with *many men* as judges; Esther is among *many* women confronted in *female space* with *one man* as judge. In both circumstances, the females are unveiled and implicitly exposed before males who are not male blood relatives (patrikin) and are not husbands, thus threatening the female sense of shame—their perception of their own reputations. Vashti refuses to defer to her husband, protecting her shame; and she is summarily dismissed from her title and from the narrative, never to be heard of again. Esther, unlike Vashti, does not protest; it is implied that she is obedient to her patrikin when she reveals her beauty to the king.[25] Certainly Vashti is confronted with a much more shaming situation; but Esther is also faced with behavior not in accord with her (Jewish) values. The connotation is that women should obey their patrikin or husbands even if their shame is threatened. Female obedience to male authority is shown to be preferable to insistence on established communal values.

The modesty code of feminine shame requires discriminating women to deny sexual interests and to avoid men who are not kin, by not allowing themselves to be seen by men and by acting and dressing to avoid drawing attention to their beauty.[26] The beauty contest—suggested by the servants to find Ahasuerus a mate—violates the values of honor/shame more blatantly than Vashti's refusal does, but in ways that dishonor the women, not the men.

Esther's deference to Mordecai's command that she not "reveal her people or her kindred" (2:10) is consonant with loyalties in patricentered systems: the women remain bound to their patrikin even in marriage.[27] Mordecai, as the responsible patrikin, is sufficiently concerned about his charge that he "walked to and fro every day [for twelve months!] in front of the court of the women's quarters in order to learn of Esther's welfare and what would be done to her" (2:11). Mordecai's perambulations emphasize the normally strict separation of male and female spaces and make the king's command to Vashti to appear among the men seem all the more capricious. Similarly, Esther's "modesty" in this immodest situation is underscored by passivity: in 2:8, Esther "was brought to the king's house"; and in 2:11, Mordecai is concerned with "what will become of her."

After a twelve-month period of beautification, each young woman "goes in to" the king, leaving the women's quarters in the evening and returning in the morning (2:13-14). There is no doubt that a sexual encounter takes place, that the virgins return to the women's quarters unsuitable for marriage or any alliance outside the king's harem.[28] The honor/shame of life in the king's harem may excuse the loss of shame the virgins suffer and even justify unchaste sex for a Jewess living in exile.[29] Esther is spared this dilemma by being chosen queen and duly married, albeit to a non-Jew. Recognizing a preference for low public profile as exiled Jews (shame) and outward assimilation with the dominant culture (honor) clarifies Esther's un-Jewish behavior and explains Mordecai's cautioning Esther to keep her Jewish heritage secret.

With the king's choice of Esther as his queen, mention is first made of Mordecai's sitting "in the king's gate" (2:19), an honorific position. The very next verse (2:20) reminds the reader that Esther has not revealed herself as a Jew because "Esther obeyed the command of Mordecai, as she did when she was supported by him." As expected, despite her marriage to the king, Esther's primary loyalties remain with her patrikin.

Mordecai's newly augmented honor positions him to overhear the plot of two eunuchs against the king. Surely the fact that eunuchs—feminized, hence nonautonomous "males"—are plotting against the king, the epitome of male power, suggests that the "normal" honor/shame values of the community are ironically skewed. Curiously, despite the strict separation earlier, Mordecai is somehow able to relate the plot directly to the queen: there is no mention of transmission by messenger (2:22). Esther, still modest and obedient, gives credit to Mordecai and does not assert herself in relaying the message. Significantly, at this juncture there also seems to be no problem with direct access to the king: "And Esther told the king in Mordecai's name" (2:22). The culprits are punished, and the events are "written in the book of the chronicles before [*liphnê*, "in the face of"] the king" (2:23). The presence of the king emphasizes his knowledge and approval of the entry.[30]

Jews (Mordecai) versus Amalekites (Haman)

The king's leadership is immediately brought into question when he elevates not Mordecai, who has saved his life, but Haman, the son of Hammedatha the Agagite. Like Mordecai, Haman is provided with a genealogy and family identification, one that invokes the enmity between their respective peoples—Jews and Amalekites.[31] (It also implicitly differentiates between Haman the Agagite and the Persian ruler in whose kingdom he resides.) It is against the background of Mordecai's life-saving deed that the king, without any apparent grounds for doing so, honors Haman to sit over all the other courtiers, who must now bow and worship him.[32]

This action increases Haman's honor vis-à-vis Mordecai (and all the other courtiers); but Mordecai, unlike the other courtiers, refuses to recognize Haman's position. Mordecai apparently justifies his refusal by identifying himself as a Jew (3:4). Haman responds by including *all* the Jews in his revenge: he "scorned to lay hand on Mordecai alone, for they had revealed to him the people of Mordecai" (3:6).

What is it that necessitates Mordecai's abandoning his well-preserved public anonymity? Nothing less than his perception that his honor has been affronted. Esther may lose her shame, but Mordecai the Jew will not bow before an Amalekite, the prototypical enemy of the Jew.[33] The effect is that Mordecai the Jew refuses to acknowledge the position of Haman the Amalekite, implying that the latter is a lesser man. Haman is enraged that his honor is decried and decides to revenge himself not only on Mordecai but also on all Jews. Mordecai has publicly shamed Haman; and Haman seeks to avenge himself by destroying Mordecai and his entire people, thereby reasserting his (Haman's) honor in the eyes of the community.

In response to Haman's complaint against "a certain people" and promised economic advantage, the king takes off the royal ring, his seal of authority, and gives it to Haman.[34] The king has acceded without question and without verification (a form of control) of Haman's claims, with "feminine" impulsiveness instead of "masculine" consideration. By handing over the royal ring, the authority that the king has consistently been ambivalent about exercising is symbolically relinquished, again bringing his autonomy (honor) into question, and establishing the lax ("feminine," as opposed to "masculine" control) manner with which the king exercises the authority of his position. The royal signet ring and power of decree, symbol of consummate masculine autonomy, is ceded to one of lesser degree in a paradoxically "feminine" reaction.

A few verses later, Haman issues commands to the king's lieutenants and to the provincial governors. The runners are hurried out by the "king's word [commandment]" (3:15), for the king's seal ring proclaims the king's word, even if it originates with someone else. (The linguistic motif of "hurry" links Haman's rise and fall: here he hurries others with the power of the king's ring; later, he will be hurried.) With Haman's word under the king's seal, the two men—the king, a leader shamed by his lack of autonomy, and Haman, a subject who "leads" the king—sit down to drink. Once again, drink is associated with the king's inappropriate want of autonomy.

To this point in the narrative, Mordecai has represented the honor/shame of the assimilated Israelites, and Ahasuerus has exemplified the paradoxically foolish (shamed) leader (honored) of the Persians. With the crisis precipitated by Haman's actions against the Jews, these roles shift: Mordecai's autonomy seems displaced to Esther, who acts autonomously but modestly, never seeking the male prerogative of public honor; and Haman usurps the role of shame, surpassing and, by comparison, somewhat redeeming the Persian king.

Esther Honors Shame

Mordecai's response to the warrant for genocide is to shame himself openly by tearing his clothes, by putting on sackcloth and ashes, and by crying publicly, loudly and bitterly (4:1). Esther's reaction is dramatic: "she writhed in pain exceedingly" (4:4) and immediately sends clothing to reassert his honor; for Mordecai's abasing himself shames not only himself but also his family, including Esther. After all, with Mordecai's self-abasement, Esther's kinship male-authority figure has been made weak, "feminized." This creates a paradoxical position for Esther: she is outwardly honored as queen and inwardly shamed by her uncle's shame. Naturally, she seeks to restore honor to her uncle (and herself) by sending him proper clothing.[35] It is also clear that, in the protection of the harem, Esther does not know of Haman's and Ahasuerus's edicts against the Jews and the cause of Mordecai's shaming himself.

Upon Mordecai's refusal, Esther gives Hathach the eunuch an order (*ṣwh*) to ascertain the reason for Mordecai's aberrant behavior, confirming that she does not know of the edict (4:5). Despite self-dishonor, Mordecai retains authority; he uses a string of verbs and verbal phrases directed to Esther: "give," "show," "declare," "command," "order (*ṣwh*) her to go," "make supplication," "seek help" (4:8). Esther's response gives Hathach the eunuch an order (*ṣwh*) to deliver a message to Mordecai but does not command her relative; she merely reminds Mordecai (and informs the reader) of the danger involved in appearing before the king without express summons (4:9). Mordecai abandons honor but retains authority; Esther assumes authority but maintains deference. Consistent with the established separation of authorized male and female spaces, all communication between Esther and Mordecai is not direct but through a eunuch—a "safe" demi-male—as messenger. Mordecai does not risk approaching Esther but wants Esther to approach the king. An element of ruthlessness—or is it disdain for women?—in Mordecai's character may be inferred.

Although Esther protests that she cannot approach the king without his having called for her, the narrative shows that she has approached him earlier to tell him of Mordecai's discovery of the plot (2:22) without any mention of the scepter of approval. Is this a device to increase narrative tension? This conjecture seems validated by Esther's descriptive emphasis on what is assumed to be common knowledge about the rules of the inner court. Along with increased suspense, this narrative tactic also allows the danger of Esther's mission to ennoble her.

Initially, Mordecai interprets Esther's response as refusal. He maintains his "command" (*ṣwh*) form (4:13) to the eunuch(s) and uses a threatening tone to Esther, even implying that her role as queen may have the intrinsic purpose of saving the Jews from this predicament (4:14). Esther then breaks the series of "orders," using the milder "speak" (*'mr*) to direct the messengers; and this time her words, without specific mention of command (*ṣwh*), do convey an imperative to Mordecai: "Go, gather . . . and fast" (4:16). These astute variations toy with autonomy and dependence—honor and shame.

Subtly, Esther maintains her feminine "shame" even as she assumes increased responsibility. I suggest that she manages this by shifting her allegiance from Mordecai to a higher male authority, God. Although God is never mentioned in this book, Esther summons a traditional avenue of prayer and supplication: fasting, including abstinence from all drink.[36] She asks all the Jews to fast for her, as she will do with her maidens, for three days. Offering the epitome of effacement, Esther is willing to surrender her own life for the sake of the community, to save her people: "If I die, I die" (4:16). Mordecai's response is to do "all that Esther had commanded him" (4:17). In paradoxical tandem, Esther remains outwardly deferential, but Mordecai acknowledges her power.

Despite her autonomous decision, Esther does not act as an independent agent. She ritualizes by fasting and communalizes by involving all the people and her maidens at the court. These are Jewish responses to be tacitly compared with the banquets, especially with the nonritualized, unrestrained drinking of the Persians. The apparatus of honor/shame suggests that power and honor do not shift from Mordecai to Esther; they pass from Mordecai to a greater power through whom Esther works. Esther's response subtly compares the Jewish greater power with the Persian kingly power, to the detriment of the Persian ruler of the Jews.

Esther dresses herself in royal clothing for her unexpected visit to the king. By so doing, she calls attention to her beauty and her sexual appeal, not denying them in the manner of feminine modesty and shame. It seems that individual abuses of honor/shame may be acceptable but communal honor must be maintained.[37] This behavior can be seen as a paradigm for the Jews in exile.

Ahasuerus assumes that there is a request (*baqqāšāh*) attached to Esther's appearance and makes exaggerated promises. The beautifully dressed (shameless) Esther answers with extreme modesty (shame), seeking the king's approval ("if [it seems] good to the king" [5:4]) before inviting him and Haman to a banquet prepared for him.[38] This banquet, unlike the earlier ones, is private, in the queen's quarters, and prepared by Esther herself, thereby reinforcing her feminine shame by acting as "servant" to the men.[39] Ahasuerus sends a message to hurry (*mhr*) Haman to do the queen's bidding, which subtly shifts authority from the king to his queen: Haman is to follow the directives of a woman. Since it is "inappropriate" for a "dominant" male to be commanded by a "submissive" female, the narrative discreetly ridicules Haman.[40]

At the banquet, Ahasuerus once again seeks to learn what Esther will ask, her petition (*šᵉ'lāh*); and he repeats his exaggerated promises. As before, the king's hyperbole is an effective contrast with Esther's even more humbled response. This time, two conditional subjunctive phrases ("If I have found favor in the eyes of the king," and "if [it seems] good to the king" [5:8]) precede her petition (*šᵉ'lāh*) and her request (*baqqāšāh*), which is for their attendance at a second banquet that Esther will prepare. Esther concludes her request by submitting her authority to the king's: she will act "according to the king's word" (5:8). Esther's words and actions all support her claim to shame. They also draw attention to the authority of the king's word, providing a foil for his actions.

With the king's acquiescence implied, the narrative shifts temporarily to an omniscient point of view. Until now, it has been objective, rendering what could be seen or heard but offering no inner feelings or thoughts. Suddenly the reader is invited to perceive Haman's shifting inner responses to the honor of a second invitation and to Mordecai's refusal to honor him. This brief change of perspective allows the reader to experience Haman's barely controlled fury and, since control is tantamount to autonomy, Haman's equivocal honor. Once more objective, the narrative shows Haman at home with his wife and friends, to whom he brags about the various kinds of honor he has accrued, culminating in Esther's banquets. He flaunts the fact that Esther herself prepares them and that he is the only (outside) man invited. Ironically, Haman depicts himself as honored by a woman's invitation to table. Even as he claims honor, he diminishes that honor.

Yet all the honor "avails [Haman] nothing" in the light of Mordecai's presence at the king's gate (5:9). Mordecai's refusal to honor Haman, in fact, effectively counters all the honor Haman has received and evokes shame. Haman does not know how to thwart Mordecai; only advice from his wife and his friends generates a pleasing plan of action (to build an execution scaffold). The advice Haman takes is primarily from his wife, named first and followed by "his friends" (5:14), pointedly in reverse order from an earlier passage (5:1). It is implicitly shameful that a man rely on his wife for advice about public matters; thus the narrative shames Haman even as it displays his pride. Haman's reliance on the advice of others is consistent with that of a group-oriented, honor/shame-motivated person, who "simply needs another continually in order to know who he or she really is. . . . Such persons internalize and make their own what others say, do, and think about them because they believe it is necessary . . . to live out the expectations of others."[41]

In a shift of scene (6:1-4), Ahasuerus's sleeplessness, which he seeks to relieve by being read to from the chronicle records, makes him aware of Mordecai's honorable action in protecting the king. Even this event slyly pokes fun at the king. Although it was written "to his face," this most honored figure in the land commended someone else and only now, inadvertently, recognizes the need to reward. Ahasuerus has to ask what has been done to honor and dignify Mordecai. The implication is that he does not know what is going on in his palace, let alone in his kingdom. Ahasuerus's dependence is stressed by his immediately seeking advice when he learns that Mordecai has not been rewarded: "'Nothing has been done for him [Mordecai].' And the king said, 'Who [is] in the court?'" (6:3b-4). The king's leadership—honor—has been consistently presented ironically.

Situational irony adds zest to the developments. Haman happens to be in the outer court, seeking permission to hang Mordecai on the newly constructed scaffold, when Ahasuerus consults him on how to honor "the man whom the king wants to honor" (6:6). Haman naturally thinks he is to be honored, so he advises public recognition—essential to honor—in the king's robes, attired by "one of the king's most noble courtiers" (6:9). There is no royal consideration or evaluation: the king impetuously wants the advice he has received followed immediately—"Hurry!" (*mhr*)—as he earlier directed Haman to hurry (*mhr*) to come to Esther's banquet, another subtle erosion of his honor.

The irony becomes multidimensional when Haman, as "one of the king's most noble courtiers," must dress Mordecai, lead him through the streets and proclaim him as recipient of the king's honor. Haman's honor as a noble courtier actually shames him when he must honor Mordecai, his enemy. The Mordecai-Haman (Jew-Amalekite) opposition is reinforced when Mordecai returns to the king's gate, royally attired, but Haman "hurried to his house mourning" (6:12), just as Mordecai was earlier in the mourning attire of sackcloth and ashes and Haman was honored by the king. Even Haman's counselors, his friends and his wife, predict Haman's defeat "if Mordecai [is] of the seed of the Jews" (6:13). With these words, the narrative foreshadows the culminating triumph—honor—of the Jews. In so doing, the opposition of good (Mordecai, Jews) and evil (Haman, Amalekites) avoids directly involving the Persian kingdom in which the Jews are exiled. Ahasuerus may be diffident and impetuous, but he is not associated with evil.

With this prognosis of doom from his wife and friends, Haman is rushed by the king's eunuchs to Esther's banquet. The delightful play on honor/shame ironically represents Haman's "honor" as he is being "hurried"—without the autonomy of his own time—by eunuchs to a woman's banquet. He does not enter alone; the king must accompany him to Esther's quarters in the restricted women's area of the palace.

As before, the king seeks to know Esther's request (*bqš*) and makes promises of generosity. Esther's long-postponed enunciation of her wish is preceded by two deferential phrases similar to the ones she used at her earlier banquet (7:3), and this time her wish is not directed toward the narrow sphere of her two guests, Ahasuerus and Haman. In a surprising shift from the inner, woman's sphere to the outer, political, male sphere, Esther pleads for her people, all the Jews exiled in Persia. In answer to the king's query after her request (*baqqāšāh*), Esther personalizes and dramatizes her wish by first asking for her own life by petition (*š'l*) and then for the life of her people by request (*baqqāšāh*). She identifies her people with herself, as queen and as the king's beloved, by saying "*We* are sold, my people and I" (7:4). The planned genocide is dramatically tripled in expression: "to be destroyed, to be killed, and to perish" (7:4). In conclusion, Esther emphasizes her humility (shame) by insisting she would not speak were they to be sold as slaves, as Haman had slyly implied. even though the damage to the king would far exceed the reparations (the ten thousand talents of silver paid by Haman) made by the enemy.[42]

The king naturally wants to know whose heart is so filled (with pride, self-honor) to do this. Esther again triples her answer and adds a fourth expression, surpassing the three forms of death with four qualities of the enemy: "A man, an enemy, a hater—Haman! This evil [one]" (7:6). Implicitly, Esther has identified herself as a Jew, and she has done so without permission from Mordecai, her patrikin. She apparently acts on her own initiative, but humbly, seeking no honor for herself. Indeed, Esther's decisiveness (power, honor) coupled with humility (shame) is in sharp contrast to masculine indecisiveness (Ahasuerus) and pride (Haman). Even Mordecai is powerless to protect the Jews. This woman—whose traditional claim to (vicarious) honor is through feminine shame and by ennobling her male kinsmen—achieves what her patrikin cannot. Paradoxically, Esther gains honor through her opportune practice of shame.

The king's response is consistent with his character. Without an able advisor nearby to tell him what to do, he does nothing—that is, he seeks to vent his anger by leaving the scene and walking in the palace garden. When he returns, he misinterprets Haman's prostrating himself before the queen as "ravishing" her; and, to add to the affront, Haman has not even waited until the king has left the house. The king not only jumps to conclusions that offend his honor but, consistent with his character, does not investigate his suspicions, voicing what appears to be a purely rhetorical question (7:8). Ahasuerus's impetuous response contributes to his image as ineffectual ("feminine") even as it reinforces the honor/shame values of the culture.

Instead of improving his situation, Haman has insured his own demise. It is noteworthy that Haman, who was brought into the queen's quarters by the king, has his face *covered* to leave.[43] The strict exclusion of the harem, broken only on Esther's request, is restored, and Haman's right to sight of forbidden (female) spaces is revoked. The royal anger is not dispelled until, at the recommendation of a eunuch, Haman is hanged on the scaffold he had prepared for Mordecai.

Ahasuerus does give Haman's house to Esther, but this narrated action does not permit knowledge of the king's dependence or autonomy. On the other hand, Mordecai is invited to appear before the king because "Esther had told what he was to her" (8:1). Esther had earlier revealed herself as a Jew; now she reveals her relationship to Mordecai—again apparently autonomously. The king, consistently impetuous, gives Mordecai the ring (and the honor) that he had withdrawn from Haman. Ahasuerus apparently relinquishes his authority and his honor rather lightly, which emphasizes once again his impotence, his inadequacy, his deficiency in honor, as leader.[44] Indeed, it is Esther, not Ahasuerus, who "set[s] Mordecai over the house of Haman" (8:2).

Esther's power (honor) is quickly and characteristically mitigated by humility (shame) as she prostrates herself before the king (8:3).[45] Her deference to the king's authority is heightened by her tears as she "begs favor" of him to countermand Haman's plot. Significantly, Haman, whose name has not been otherwise qualified since 3:1, is suddenly and consistently referred to as "Haman the Agagite" or "Haman the son of Hammedatha the Agagite," which emphasizes Haman's role as prototypical enemy of the Jews and also separates him from the Persian king and his people. This and the following passages subtly mark the shift of authority from Mordecai to Esther (who nevertheless remains modest) and a shift of shame from the king (who retains leadership) to Haman.

To couch her plea with utmost intensity, this time Esther uses four separate phrases of supplication: "'If it pleases the king [*shame*], and if I have found favor in his sight [*shameless*], and the thing is right before the king [*shame*], and I [am] pleasing in his eyes [*shameless*]'" (8:5).

To her modest (shame) phrases, Esther adds clear reminders of her (sexual) appeal to Ahasuerus, including a "shameless" coda recalling the earlier and less pronounced "if I have found favor in [the king's] sight" (7:3). Esther's clever balance of shame and shamelessness in her actions is succinctly expressed as she seeks to redress Haman's edict.

Esther wants to retrieve the letters sent by Haman with the king's authority (seal ring) to forestall the planned genocide. She personalizes her plea in terms of the pain it will cause her: "'For how will I face the evil that my people will find? And how can I face the slaughter of my kindred?'" (8:6). Esther reiterates the patriarchal kinship bond, the foundation of Jewish honor/shame cultural values, in her appeal.[46] The king responds by reiterating what he has done (given Esther Haman's house and hanged Haman) "because he [Haman] laid his hands on the Jews" (8:7), but he cannot rescind what has been written with his authority. Instead, he advises Esther and Mordecai to write for the Jews, "as it pleases" them, "in the king's name and seal it with the king's ring" (8:8). Ahasuerus's advice is an apparently autonomous move, without counsel, which begins to restore his authority and honor. His independent action avoids characterizing the king as in the power of the Jews and also emphasizes that Ahasuerus does not save the Jews; the Jews do.

The scribes are called in, but it is Mordecai, not Esther, who dictates the letters to be sent out in the name of Ahasuerus and sealed with his ring. Esther, who has employed autonomy and power to save her people, does not seem to strive for power or to accrue masculine honor for herself. She reverts to modest shame, and Mordecai increasingly resumes authority and honor.

Mordecai cannot undo the edict permitting attack on the Jews, but he can direct the Jews to assemble and to avenge (*nqm*) themselves. Haman's edict had not permitted the Jews self-defense: they were reduced to the (feminine) position of helplessness (shame), unable to protect their own families and their honor. Mordecai's edict permits them to congregate and not only defend themselves (as powerless women) but also to avenge themselves (as honorable men)—but they may kill only those who attack them, including women and children. The text suggests that if women and children assume the male prerogative of autonomous aggression, they will be treated as males. The Jews are also authorized to plunder those who are killed, just as Haman encouraged the people to plunder the Jews. Plundering is an expression of autonomy and authority over another, but the Jews decline to exercise this form of power (9:9, 16).[47]

Only when the Jewish population has been notified does Mordecai celebrate his elevated position and honor. Since honor must be recognized publicly, Mordecai's prominence is again proclaimed by public parade in royal accoutrements. Whereas the city of Susa was "troubled" with Haman's edict, it rejoices with recognition of Mordecai. The narrative repeatedly attributes unwarranted pride, honor-grabbing and enmity toward the Jews to Haman and his people, and separates those qualities from the Persian population.[48] "For the Jews there was light and gladness and joy and honor . . . the Jews had joy and gladness, a feast."[49] The Jews have honor (8:16)— autonomy and power—through Mordecai's honorific position even though they are in exile, in a dependent situation. This passage highlights a major thrust of the book: how diaspora Jews can achieve honor and autonomy within a foreign culture in which they are an ineffective—if not scorned—minority. The outward assimilation to the dominant culture is developed in the closing chapters to emphasize the cohesiveness of the Jewish community.

On schedule, on the day when "the enemies of the Jews hoped to have *power* over them," the reverse occurs, and the "Jews had *rule* over the ones who hated them" (9:1). The Jews are depicted as invincible; "no one would withstand them"; and part of their power is the people's awe of the Jews. Even the provincial ruling nobles come to the aid of the Jews, and the awe shifts from the Jews en masse to Mordecai (9:3). Symbolic leader and representative of the Jews, Mordecai personifies the people; and his honor in Susa gives honor to the people. With Mordecai's public honor, the narrative also continues the transference of honor from Esther to Mordecai so that the conclusion specifies a male symbol of honor for the patriarchal Jews. The text emphasizes that this is a struggle not only for life but also for autonomy; and the Jews, even in exile, are accorded independence and honor as they "rule over" their attackers by avenging themselves but not taking spoil (9:10).

The text celebrates the Jews' autonomy and honor in details of the narrative resolution: a round number of five hundred men "killed and destroyed" is given veracity by adding named individuals, enemies of the Jews in the palace of Susa, including the sons of Haman (9:6-10). Ahasuerus is duly notified, and suddenly, apparently without being summoned, Esther is again in the king's presence. No formality of scepter-touching occurs here (which adds to skepticism about the earlier drama). The king tells Esther what has happened in Susa and asks for her further requests. Although he does ask for information ("What have they done in the rest of the king's provinces?" [9:12]), Ahasuerus does not ask for advice and thereby retains his autonomy and honor.

This time, Esther's requests are prefaced by only one phrase of humility ("If it pleases the king" [9:13]). Perhaps this and her unsummoned appearance attest to her newly attained confidence (but not transgressing deferential shame) with her husband and king. She asks that Haman's already-dead sons be hanged in public disgrace, presumably to shame utterly the enemies of the Jews; and that the following day also be designated for the Jews' avenging themselves against their enemies. Her request is granted. Three hundred enemy men are killed in Susa on the second day and an additional seventy-five thousand in the provinces; and again the Jews "did not lay their hands on the spoil" (9:16). To celebrate their deliverance with honor, the Jews feast in Susa and in the provinces and establish the fourteenth of Adar as a day "of sending portions to one another" (9:19). No mention of drink is made, and the nonredistributive feasts of the opening chapter are rectified to correspond with Jewish tradition.

Mordecai is given the recognition—honor—of being literate (9:20, 23) and of establishing a holiday to celebrate deliverance "by sending portions to one another and gifts to the poor" (9:22). Whereas scribes wrote all the messages for Ahasuerus and Haman, the text explicitly states that Mordecai himself wrote about the events and sent letters to the Jews in outlying areas of the kingdom, and that Esther and Mordecai wrote "to confirm this second letter of Purim." Against the background of Ahasuerus's questionable literacy, the Jewish community is honored through its learned (symbolic) leaders. In this milieu of honor/shame, it is notable that Esther is given equal credit with Mordecai for writing (that is, for literacy and authority); and that the "decree of Esther" (9:32) accords her a distinctly "masculine" (public and legal) role. Esther *receives* (feminine) rather than *seeks* (masculine) recognition, once again merging honor/shame without blurring their distinctive functions.

Structurally, the festivities of the Jewish deliverance *correspond* to and *reverse* those of the Persian introduction: public honor, feasts, sending messages, distributing portions; but whereas honor/shame are initially polarized, they are merged in some characters and shared between the sexes in various degrees by the conclusion. Only the "appearance" of honor/shame remains paradigmatic for females. Esther retains the demeanor of female shame even as she invokes honor.

After a recapitulation explaining the origin of Purim (9:20-28), both Esther the queen and Mordecai the Jew are recognized for their deeds, and a "decree of Esther" confirms the ritual observance (9:29-32). In the concluding chapter, even King Ahasuerus is redeemed. He makes decisions without recourse to advisors ("laid a tax") and his "acts of . . . authority and of his might" (10:2) give him honor, adding complexity to his earlier shame. The king's honor is underscored by the honor given to the "greatness of Mordecai" by the king: "For Mordecai the Jew was second to King Ahasuerus, and great among the Jews, and pleasing to his many kinsmen,[50] seeking the welfare of his people and speaking peace to all his seed" (10:3). Esther, for whom the book is named, is not mentioned in the concluding verse. Instead, Mordecai, who depends on Esther in the crisis he himself causes by his refusal to bend his pride (and his knees) to honor Haman, is restored to his place as dominant male with all due honor. Esther, as a modest female who protects her shame when possible and is shameless when necessary, is once again subsumed in Mordecai's honor.

Honor/shame permeates the action in the Book of Esther and offers substantive support for reading the book as a paradigm for the Jewish diaspora. Paradoxically, the narrative supports and satirizes sexual politics through an intelligent and resourceful woman who uses—and abuses—the system to achieve her purpose: to allay threats to the existence of the community of Jews and restore to their lives a sense of autonomy within dependence. This interpretation teaches that Jews in a dependent position in exile can maintain their honor by *outwardly* observing the customs and laws of the host country while still maintaining their communal solidarity. Thus the *appearance* of feminine shame masks Esther's actions in the masculine world just as Mordecai's *appearance* of feminine shame is actually an action of masculine power directed to involve Esther. The text allows that, in threatening situations, social paradigms may be creatively interpreted as long as the prescribed gender role is publicly observed. Powerless women—and Jews—can invoke power as long as they maintain required appearances.

Esther has been championed as an example of an enterprising woman. Nevertheless, the text demonstrates how she acts behind the mask of "feminine shame." Thus Esther epitomizes the book's message and manipulation of the honor/shame theme.

Abbreviations

AB	Anchor Bible
ABRL	Anchor Bible Reference Library
BDB	Brown, Driver, Briggs, *A Hebrew and English Lexicon of the Old Testament*
BHS	*Biblia Hebraica Stuttgartensia*
BibLitSer	Bible and Literature Series
BibSem	Biblical Seminar
BZAW	Beihefte zur Zeitschrift für die alttestamentliche Wissenschaft
CBC	Cambridge Bible Commentary
CSHJ	Chicago Studies in the History of Judaism
EvQ	*Evangelical Quarterly*
FCB	Feminist Companion to the Bible
Gesenius	Wilhelm Gesenius, *A Hebrew and English Lexicon of the Old Testament*
HUCA	*Hebrew Union College Annual*
Int	*Interpretation*
ISBL	Indiana Studies in Biblical Literature
JBL	*Journal of Biblical Literature*
JPS	*Tanakh: The Holy Scriptures—The New Jewish Publication Society Translation According to the Traditional Hebrew Text*
JSOT	*Journal for the Study of the Old Testament*

JSOTSup	Journal for the Study of the Old Testament Supplement Series
KJV	King James Version
LBS	Library of Biblical Studies
LXX	Septuagint
NEB	New English Bible
NIV	New International Version
OBT	Overtures to Biblical Theology
RSV	Revised Standard Version
SBL	Society of Biblical Literature
SBT	Studies in Biblical Theology
VT	*Vetus Testamentum*

Notes

Preface

1. Harold Bloom and David Rosenberg, *The Book of J* (New York: Vintage, 1991).

2. Athalya Brenner, "Women Poets and Authors," in *The Feminist Companion to the Bible, I: The Song of Songs,* ed. Athalya Brenner (Sheffield: Sheffield Academic, 1993), 865–97. See also Susan Ackerman's *Warrior, Dancer, Seductress, Queen: Women in Judges and Biblical Israel,* ABRL (New York: Doubleday, 1998), 261ff., for the possibility of women's voices in other song sequences.

3. Interlinear Bibles offer valuable assistance to readers who are not fluent in Hebrew. See, for example, Jay P. Green Sr., ed. and trans., *The Interlinear Bible: Hebrew/English,* vols. I–III (Grand Rapids: Baker, 1983); John R. Kohlenberger III, ed., *The NIV Interlinear Hebrew-English Old Testament* (Grand Rapids: Zondervan, 1987).

Introduction

1. The examples provided in this chapter intentionally avoid referring to the text of the following chapters.

2. For example, the deaths of Naomi and Ruth (Ruth 4) are not mentioned, nor that of Hannah (1 Samuel 21) or Rahab (Joshua 2 and 6).

3. Norman K. Gottwald suggests that the "*stigmatization of menstruation* as a 'blemish' strengthened the *marginalization of women* in public and cultic roles . . ." (Gottwald's italics); *The Hebrew Bible: A Socio-Literary Introduction* (Philadelphia: Fortress Press, 1985), 478.

4. See Lila Abu-Lughod, *Veiled Sentiments: Honor and Poetry in a Bedouin Society* (Berkeley: University of California Press, 1986); but see Carol Meyers, *Discovering Eve: Ancient Israelite Women in Context* (Oxford: Oxford Univ. Press, 1988), for another opinion.

5. Ruth is the widowed daughter-in-law of Naomi. Through Ruth, Naomi becomes the ancestress of David, king of Israel.

6. See Lillian R. Klein, *The Triumph of Irony in the Book of Judges,* JSOTSup 68 (Sheffield: Sheffield Academic, 1988), 111–15.

7. See Adele Reinhartz, *Why Ask My Name? Anonymity and Identity in Biblical Narrative* (Oxford: Oxford Univ. Press, 1998); Carol L. Meyers, Ross S. Kraemer, and Toni Craven, eds., *Women in Scripture: A Dictionary of Named and Unnamed Women in the Hebrew Bible, the Apocryphal/Deuterocanonical Books, and the New Testament* (Boston: Houghton Mifflin, 2000).

8. There are other possible justifications for Michal's childlessness, but David's unavailability is certainly a strong possibility.

9. See Klein, *Triumph of Irony,* 30–33.

10. A selection of nontheological studies: Gottwald, *The Hebrew Bible;* Joel Rosenberg, *King and Kin: Political Allegory in the Hebrew Bible,* ISBL (Bloomington: Indiana Univ. Press, 1986); Howard Eilberg-Schwartz, *The Savage in Judaism: An Anthropology of Israelite Religion and Ancient Judaism* (Bloomington: Indiana Univ. Press, 1990); Mark S. Smith, *The Early History of God: Yahweh and the Other Deities in Ancient Israel,* 2nd ed. (Grand Rapids: Eerdmans, 2002); Robert Alter and Frank Kermode, eds., *The Literary Guide to the Bible* (Cambridge: Harvard Univ. Press, 1987); Meir Sternberg, *The Poetics of Biblical Narrative: Ideological Literature and the Drama of Reading,* ISBL (Bloomington: Indiana Univ. Press, 1985).

11. Greek mythologies also try to circumvent the female presence in reproduction.

Chapter 1

A Feminist Companion to Judges, ed. Athalya Brenner, FCB 4 (Sheffield: Sheffield Academic, 1993), 25–33, 55–71.

1. A random sample: Phyllis Trible, *Texts of Terror: Literary-Feminist Readings of Biblical Narratives,* OBT (Philadelphia: Fortress Press, 1984; Athalya Brenner, *The Israelite Woman: Social Role and Literary Type in Biblical Narrative,* BibSem 2 (Sheffield: JSOT Press, 1985); Mieke Bal, *Lethal Love: Feminist*

Literary Readings of Biblical Love Stories, ISBL (Bloomington: Indiana Univ. Press, 1987). The single book addressing the women in Judges at this date is Bal's *Death and Dissymetry: The Politics of Coherence in the Book of Judges,* CSHJ (Chicago: University of Chicago Press, 1988), which explores "the relations between text and social reality" as it concerns women's lives and deaths.

2. The values proposed are limited to the Book of Judges; other biblical books may contradict these values. The Book of Ruth, for instance, is much more liberal regarding foreign women.

3. Admittedly, these are the ethics and morality common to the Judeo-Christian culture, which may or may not be valid for the Philistines.

4. Since all the women negatively presented are sexually mature and active, relative age must, in this case, be deduced from the context. Jael and Micah's mother are paired by the nature of their deeds, and in this pairing, Jael's seductive behavior suggests she is the younger of the two.

5. The outcome is finally disastrous for the Philistines, but only after a series of intervening and determining events. Samson's love of Delilah is in itself adverse for Israel and beneficial to the Philistines.

6. Perhaps even multiple marriages of men.

7. Lillian R. Klein, *The Triumph of Irony in the Book of Judges,* JSOTSup 68 (Sheffield, England: Almond, 1988).

8. The several interim females vary from these polarities in some degree; even Deborah, otherwise faultless, is handicapped as a military leader by virtue of her being a woman.

9. Hebrew root *syt,* Hiphil: urge, incite, induce, persuade (Benjamin Davidson, *The Analytical Hebrew and Chaldee Lexicon* [Peabody, Mass.: Hendrickson, 1984], 575); invite, allure, instigate (BDB, 694).

10. BDB, 540.

11. A somewhat more forceful reading is found in the RSV: "she urged him to ask her father for a field."

12. C. F. Burney, *The Book of Judges,* LBS (New York: Ktav, 1970), 13.

13. Avrohom Fishelis and Shmuel Fishelis, *Judges: A New English Translation* (New York: Judaica, 1979), 5.

14. Women can—and do—act outside the patriarchal constraints, without male approval, or can also be entirely passive. The text suggests women are encouraged to act, but within the system, with male approval.

15. Such "stimulating behavior" outside marriage was considered seductive and severely reproved as luring males away from their nobler interests. The

single woman could—and should—withhold her sexual favors. The married woman probably could not.

16. Were the sequence reversed, it would suggest the woman's moving from one relationship to the other, from father-daughter to husband-wife.

17. *Tiṣnah* is usually interpreted as "to descend," inferred from the text. See BDB, 856; Gesenius, 688.

18. I can discover no basis for inferring Delilah to be Israelite, and there is at least the suggestion that she is Philistine. After his disdain of his parent's charge that he find a woman of his own people and his subsequent escapades with non-Israelite women (the Timnite woman and the prostitute of Gaza), Samson's love for Delilah and her association with Philistines are consistent with his earlier behavior, all of which strongly supports that she is not an Israelite and is a Philistine.

19. Thus the narrative lures the reader into judging Delilah outside her cultural group, by standards not necessarily applicable to the character.

20. For the "key term" concept with regard to this passage, see Jacob Licht, *Storytelling in the Bible* (Jerusalem: Magnes, 1978), 60.

21. Established among the Canaanites; presumed among the Philistines. See Niels Peter Lemche, *Ancient Israel: A New History of Israelite Society,* Bib-Sem 5 (Sheffield: Sheffield Academic, 1988), 207–8.

22. Davidson, *Hebrew and Chaldee Lexicon,* 26.

23. Sheldon H. Blank identifies the biblical oath as a "conditional curse"; "Curse, Blasphemy, Spell and Oath," *HUCA* 33 (1950–51): 73–95.

24. "You shall not take the name of YHWH your God in vain" (Exod. 20:7a); "Honor your father and your mother" (20:12); "You shall not steal" (20:15).

25. Even Deborah, who apparently acts on her own initiative, is actually taking orders from YHWH.

26. Parenting may be shared with the extended family, brothers of the father acting as surrogate in a patrilineal system. This functions only when an extended family is at hand, of which there is no evidence in this narrative. See Norman K. Gottwald, *The Tribes of Yahweh: A Sociology of the Religion in Liberated Israel, 1250–1050 B.C.E.* (Maryknoll, N.Y.: Orbis, 1979), 300–301.

27. For a differing but not contradictory study of "Women in the Cult," see the chapter by Mayer. I. Gruber so titled in Jacob Neusner, Baruch A. Levine and Ernest S. Frerichs, eds., *Judaic Perspectives on Ancient Israel* (Philadelphia: Fortress Press, 1987), 35–48.

Chapter 2

1. "Honey" is mentioned thirty-nine times in the Bible, often referring to date honey; "honeycomb" an additional nine times.

2. Heinrich Margulies, "Das Rätsel der Biene im Alten Testament," *VT* 24 (1974): 48.

3. This great goddess created a son without the need of a phallus; she created out of herself the first male as her son, Ophion, the snake. The son became his mother's lover but could not become her master; when he demanded participation in authority, the mother-lover chopped his head off. This reflects in symbol and myth the prevalent human understanding of the earth's eternal capacity to create and destroy its products in spring and fall.

Of the many analogies with this parallel between nature and human existence, that of the bees was the most telling. This "natural" social structure is ruled by the queen bee, who is served by a hierarchy of female bees. This reduces the males to passive drones living on the products of the female society and forming a reservoir for the annual selection of a single impregnator. The act of fertilization involves castration of the male, for the queen takes the male genitals with her, and the "winner" of this contest dies immediately after fulfilling his single independent function. In the cells prepared by her "vestal virgins," the queen returns to lay the eggs from which the next queen will arise. The superfluous male drones are killed and cleaned out of the hive by the females.

The Cretan worshipers of the Mother Goddess took this image in nature as a model for humans. The Great *Melissa,* or priest-queen, had a hierarchy of Melissa priestesses as servants of purity. Men functioned as servants of the female society and not as their masters—as subjects of the Great Melissa until one was chosen for a "secret marriage" culminating in the death of the consort. And "Melissa" in Hebrew is "Deborah."

In a land of distinctly patriarch-oriented nomads the symbol of the "queen bee" was in direct opposition to the symbol of the "shepherd of the flock" and references to the bee were repugnant. "No one has a good word to say about the bee" (Margulies, "Das Rätsel der Biene," 48).

In the patriarchal version of creation, the earth and mankind were created by a masculine figure without the benefit of a female womb: in Genesis 2 Adam is born into a womanless world and named "Adam" after the ground, the land, 'adāmāh. The land, not woman, has the feminine version of this name for man.

The word for woman has nothing to do with the reproductive earth; it is the feminine form (*'iššāh*) of an abstract word for man (*'iš*). The role of the woman in Hebraic tradition is neither the Babylonian, to sexually serve the male gods, nor the Aegean, to master men—but to serve them. Naturally, the servant has no right to demand or to call the male master to come to her. But these are the actions of Deborah.

The name of Deborah recalls not only the woman to whom the men of the tribes come to be judged and who calls Barak to come to her, but also the Cretan queen bee. Margulies suggests that references to bees were all but eliminated from the Hebrew text in order to avoid association with the hated Cretan-Philistine cult practices (Margulies, "Das Rätsel der Biene," 75). The story of Deborah, and hence her name, could not be eliminated, but it is surrounded by male figures of fire that symbolically keep this "queen bee" within *their* limits. Bees can route men, but fire routes bees. I propose that Barak's name is historical and that the meaning of his name suggested the possibility of another name of fire, Lappidot, Deborah's husband, with which to master the dreaded feminine image.

4. "Flash of lightning" is also a possible meaning for "Lappidot," but that the two men are one and the same is considered unlikely.

5. Esther may direct Mordecai's activity, but she is actually being compliant with his request (Esth 4:16).

6. In Hebrew, the text uses the infinitive absolute for emphasis: *hālōk 'ēlēk*.

7. This is a curious situation indeed. The Kenites have been closely associated with the Israelites, even with Moses himself; but Heber is apparently friendly with a long-standing enemy of the Israelites. Jael is married to someone friendly with the enemy. To whom does her allegiance belong?

Chapter 3

"Hannah: Marginalized Victim and Social Redeemer," in *A Feminist Companion to Samuel and Kings*, ed. Athalya Brenner. FCB 5 (Sheffield: Sheffield Academic, 1994), 77–92.

1. Sarah gave Hagar to her husband as a wife for purposes of conception (Gen 16:3). In a feminist reading of Hagar, Savina J. Teubal (*Hagar the Egyptian: The Lost Traditions of the Matriarchs* [San Francisco: Harper & Row, 1990], 75–81) finds that the close relationship between Hagar and Sarah is undermined by Abraham; and that, instead of conflict between two women in one household, the issue at hand is the custom of acquiring an heir, male or female,

through a woman's handmaid. I find Teubal's suggestion that the feminine bond is broken by masculine intervention an interesting parallel to the argument of this chapter.

2. One exception is the lack of envy among the women in the Song of Songs. The "daughters of Jerusalem" demonstrate no jealousy of the Shulammite maiden they themselves call the "fairest among women" (1:7; 5:9; 6:1), although Michael V. Fox suggests that they may tease her (*The Song of Songs and Ancient Egyptian Love Songs* [Madison: University of Wisconsin Press, 1985], 158); "Suspicion of that sort [jealousy] is not suggested anywhere in the Song, not even when the Shulammite mentions the love that other girls must feel for her beloved" (170).

3. "When any gesture of appropriation is imitated, it simply means that two hands will reach for the same object simultaneously: conflict cannot fail to result" (René Girard, *"To Double Business Bound": Essays on Literature, Mimesis, and Anthropology* [Baltimore: Johns Hopkins Univ. Press, 1978], 201).

4. Sacrificial scapegoats, Girard postulates, were "mimetic free-for-alls" that could terminate a disruptive mimetic crisis and reunite "the entire community against a single, powerless antagonist" (Girard, *Double Business Bound*, xii).

5. René Girard, *Things Hidden since the Foundation of the World*, trans. Stephen Bann and Michael Metteer (Stanford: Stanford Univ. Press, 1987), 288–90.

6. René Girard, *Violence and the Sacred*, trans. Patrick Gregory (Baltimore: Johns Hopkins Univ. Press, 1977), 145.

7. Girard, *Double Business Bound*, 140.

8. Girard, *Violence and the Sacred*, 146.

9. Nonacquisitive mimetic desire is considered a positive social value.

10. Marshall Sahlins, *Stone Age Economics* (Chicago: Aldine-Atherton, 1972), 198.

11. Sahlins, *Stone Age Economics*, 93.

12. Marshall Sahlins, "Exchange Value and the Diplomacy of Primitive Trade," in *Essays in Economic Anthropology Dedicated to the Memory of Karl Polanyi*, ed. June Helm, Paul Bohannan, and Marshall D. Sahlins (Seattle: University of Washington Press, 1965), 103–7.

13. For example, the serpent desires YHWH's power, the first woman desires the serpent's promised wisdom, Cain desires the divine approval Abel receives, Jacob desires Esau's birthright, Joseph's brothers desire his most-loved status.

14. The commandments that most clearly repudiate mimetic desire are: "You shall not kill" (Exod 20:7); "You shall not commit adultery" (20:8); "You

shall not steal" (20:9); "You shall not bear false witness against your neighbor" (20:16); "You shall not covet your neighbor's house; you shall not covet your neighbor's wife, or his manservant, or his maidservant, or his ox, or his ass, or anything that is your neighbor's" (20:17). Compare the equivalent commandments in Deuteronomy 5.

15. Sahlins, *Stone Age Economics*, 77.

16. But in accord with the language.

17. "A portion more" (*mānāh 'aḥat 'aphyim*). This is frequently rendered as "a double portion"; but compare the articles by Yairah Amit (68–76) and Carol Meyers (93–104) in *A Feminist Companion to Samuel and Kings*, ed. Athalya Brenner, FCB 5 (Sheffield: Sheffield Academic, 1994).

18. Esther Fuchs, "The Literary Characterization of Mothers and Sexual Politics," *Semeia* 46 (1989): 151.

19. James. G. Williams, "Between Reader and Text: A General Response," *Semeia* 46 (1989): 174. Even though Williams is referring to a "harlot" as a marginal female, the concept applies equally to Hannah, a woman at the other extreme of female marginality.

20. The simple past (without *waw*) of "for he loved Hannah" is followed by a reversal of the normal verb-noun sequence, which signals a temporal change (to past perfect) so that the following phrase reads: "and yhwh had shut up her womb" (1:5).

21. Virginia Satir, *The New Peoplemaking* (Mountain View, Calif.: Science and Behavior Books, 1988), 87.

22. Virginia Satir, *Conjoint Family Therapy*, 3rd ed. (Palo Alto, Calif.: Science and Behavior Books, 1983), 258.

23. rsv: "Why is your heart sad?"

24. Satir, *New Peoplemaking*, 87.

25. "Turns," a linguistic concept, refers to the sequence of conversational speeches. Elkanah simply speaks first, thus has the first "turn."

26. Deborah Tannen, *You Just Don't Understand: Women and Men in Conversation* (New York: Morrow, 1990), 150–52.

27. Compare Tannen, *You Just Don't Understand*, 152.

28. Tannen, *You Just Don't Understand*, 150, citing Walter Ong.

29. Compare the English translations for 1:15c.

30. In the Hebrew, ten words precede the five-word central phrase, and fourteen words follow. This structure often emphasizes the central phrase.

31. Williams, "Between Reader and Text," 177.

32. Ibid.

33. Fuchs, "Literary Characterization of Mothers," 162.

Chapter 4

"Bathsheba Revealed" in *A Feminist Companion to Samuel and Kings*, ed. Athalya Brenner. FCB 5 (Sheffield: Sheffield Academic, 1994), 47–64.

1. R. K. Harrison, "The Matriarchate and Hebrew Regal Succession," *EvQ* 29.1 (1957): 29–34. Harrison focuses on the possible influence women in the line of descent might have had in struggles for accession to the throne. Because Bathsheba, though of high birth, was not among the royal line of descent, she is not mentioned as matriarch. See also Tomoo Ishida, *The Royal Dynasties in Ancient Israel: A Study on the Formation and Development of Royal-Dynastic Ideology*, BZAW 142 (Berlin: de Gruyter, 1977); Jon D. Levenson and Baruch Halpern, "The Political Import of David's Marriages," *JBL* 99 (1980): 507–18.

2. Adele Berlin, *Poetics and Interpretation of Biblical Narrative*, BibLitSer (Sheffield: Almond, 1983), 27.

3. Shimon Bar-Efrat, *Narrative Art in the Bible*, JSOTSup 70 (Sheffield: Almond, 1989), 22–23. See earlier comments by David M. Gunn, who considers the absence of emotional content in the story (*The Story of King David: Genre and Interpretation*, JSOTSup 6 [Sheffield: JSOT Press, 1982], 99).

4. Menachem Perry and Meir Sternberg, "Gaps, Ambiguity and the Reading Process," in *The Poetics of Biblical Narrative: Ideological Literature and the Drama of Reading*, ed. Meir Sternberg, ISBL (Bloomington: Indiana Univ. Press, 1985), 186–229 (201–4); Randall C. Bailey, *David in Love and War: The Pursuit of Power in 2 Samuel 10–12*, JSOTSup 75 (Sheffield: Sheffield Academic, 1990), 89.

5. J. P. Fokkelman, *Narrative Art and Poetry in the Books of Samuel: A Full Interpretation Based on Stylistic and Structural Analyses*, vol. 1 (Assen, The Netherlands: Van Gorcum, 1981), 53; discussed by Mieke Bal, *Lethal Love: Feminist Literary Readings of Biblical Love Stories*, ISBL (Bloomington: Indiana Univ. Press, 1987), 25–29. Gale A. Yee discusses both sides in "Fraught with Background: Literary Ambiguity in II Samuel 11," *Int* 42 (1988): 243 [240–53].

6. Bal, *Lethal Love*, 23.

7. Fokkelman, "The text is moreover not at all interested in her possibly having shared the responsibility" (*Narrative Art and Poetry*, 53); Bal, "Anxiety about possible adultery seems to go against respect for the victimized woman" (*Lethal Love*, 28).

8. I am not claiming the title of "queen mother" for Bathsheba, although she has been called the first *gᵉbîrāh* and the paradigm for the senior status of the queen mother. For the pro-queen mother, see R. N. Whybray, *The Succession*

Narrative: A Study of II Samuel 9-2 and I Kings 1 and 2, SBT 2/9 (Naperville, Ill.: Allenson, 1968), 40; Ishida, *Royal Dynasties in Ancient Israel*, 142, 155–58. For a very convincing argument against, see Zafrira Ben-Barak, "The Status and Right of the *Gebirah*," in *A Feminist Companion to Samuel and Kings*, ed. Athalya Brenner, FCB 5 (Sheffield: Sheffield Academic, 1994), 170–85.

9. Perry and Sternberg, "Gaps, Ambiguity and the Reading Process," 198.

10. Randall Bailey observes that Bathsheba's "actions are not in the hiph'il verb forms, which would suggest that she was being 'caused to act.' Rather they are in the qal, she comes and returns . . . a willing and equal partner to the events which transpire" (*David in Love and War*, 88).

11. BDB, 873b.

12. Ritual uncleanness of males: Lev 5:3; 7:20, 21; 14:19; 15:3-11, 16-17, 24; Num 19:13; Lev 22:3, 5; of females: Lev 5:18-23; 25-30.

13. The mode of speech may convey an ethical quality even though both David and Bathsheba have knowingly committed adultery.

14. J. Cheryl Exum, "Bathsheba's Body 'Speaks' in an Obvious Way, Giving Her Voice," in *Fragmented Women: Feminist (Sub)versions of Biblical Narrative* (Valley Forge, Pa.: Trinity Press International, 1993), 190.

15. "Feet" is a well-known euphemism for sexual organs.

16. The word chosen to convey "gift" is derived from *nś'* (in Niphal), "be carried, be married, be lifted": ". . . and the king sent after Uriah an exaltation, a marriage from the king."

17. When the servants tell David that Uriah did not go down to his house, no mention is made of the "gift," and the verb is not "come," but "go," without sexual implications.

18. In other biblical texts (Ezekiel 16; Jeremiah 5; Deuteronomy and more) foreign males are sexually active and fertile.

19. Bailey views this as a story "of political intrigue in which sex becomes a tool of politics" (*David in Love and War*, 88).

20. Ibid.: "the narrator suggests that she is here as well as throughout the narrative a willing and equal partner to the events which transpire."

21. For a fuller discussion of this concept, see chapter 7: "Honor and Shame in the Book of Esther."

22. Of course Bathsheba's pregnancy does create a dilemma. Her husband's absence when she becomes pregnant underscores her fertility and his infertility, which further heightens the tension. Bathsheba not only cuckolds her husband but makes his infertility—his lack of manhood—public. How characteristic

that a male who cannot fulfill the essential masculine role, to fertilize, devotes himself to a militaristic career—as it were to prove his manhood.

23. John Otwell, *And Sarah Laughed: The Status of Woman in the Old Testament* (Philadelphia: Westminster, 1977), ch. 4, esp. 50.

24. James G. Williams, *Women Recounted: Narrative Thinking and the God of Israel,* BibLitSer 6 (Sheffield: Almond, 1982), 92.

25. Ibid., 107.

26. Ibid., 92.

27. Phyllis A. Bird, "Images of Women in the Old Testament," in *The Bible and Liberation: Political and Social Hermeneutics,* ed. Norman K. Gottwald (Maryknoll, N.Y.: Orbis, 1983), 252–88, esp. 268.

28. Ibid., 269.

29. The son of this conception dies, but Bathsheba and David conceive a second son, Solomon, who becomes heir to the throne.

30. Williams, *Women Recounted,* 47. Peter Miscall observes that David's male beauty "serves no obvious function in this story, although there are allusions to it in 1 Sam. 16:12 and 1 Sam. 17:42" (*1 Samuel: A Literary Reading* [Bloomington: Indiana Univ. Press, 1986], 119); Gunn and Fewell suggest female beauty "usually communicates their sexual desirability in stories of courtship, seduction or rape" and that "David's and Absalom's appearance perhaps related directly to their ability to charm" (David M. Gunn and Danna Nolan Fewell, *Narrative in the Hebrew Bible* [Oxford: Oxford Univ. Press, 1993], 57).

31. Of these "royal" women, Bathsheba and Tamar execute their plans as independent agents whereas Ruth works in concert with another woman to execute her plan.

32. Alice Bach, "The Pleasure of her Text," in Athalya Brenner, ed., *A Feminist Companion to Samuel and Kings,* FCB 5 (Sheffield: Sheffield Academic, 1994), 106–28, esp. 122.

33. "The hint of sexual impotence establishes the tone of the political scene to follow" (Gunn, *Story of King David,* 90).

34. "With the father barely dead, his two sons [quarrel] over his bed-fellow—clearly no impotence theirs!" (Gunn, *Story of King David,* 90).

35. "Nathan does not concentrate on the erotic part of David's crime, possibly because for him the appropriation of a woman, and even a married one, might have been recognized (if not necessarily approved of) as a royal prerogative. He does say, 'I [the Lord] gave you his [Saul's] kingdom and his wives' (2 Sam 12:8); nevertheless, this is of less weight in comparison to the moral crime

committed against Uriah" (Shulamit Valler, "King David and 'His' Women: Biblical Stories and Talmudic Discussions," in Brenner, *Feminist Companion to Samuel and Kings,* 140).

36. Adonijah invited "all his brothers, the king's sons, and all the royal officials of Judah, but he did not invite Nathan the prophet or Benaiah or the mighty men or Solomon his brother" (1 Kgs 1:9b).

37. Fokkelman says: "She begins by making David feel guilty, 17b-d: you have forgotten your promise and slighted your son Solomon. The reproach which follows, implying incompetence as father and king and cached in the words of v. 18, evokes a sense of failure. In 19b David will feel let down if not betrayed. Everyone, to his exclusion, is busy arranging the succession. His own sons are agitating behind his back and even his staunch friend Abiathar has deserted him. The name Joab is useful in hinting at great rancour; he is the man with more political know-how than David (2 Samuel 19:19). It is very contriving of Bathsheba to use this against Adonijah and in Solomon's favor. In v. 19c she plays on David's sympathy: Solomon is loyal to you but see how isolated he is. She continues in similar fashion in v. 21. The latter period activates a mixture of compassion (my wife and child, their last hour has struck!) and guilt feelings (how could he be so cruel as not to come to their aid). As compensation, Bathsheba puts David back on the pedestal of absolute power in v. 20 and her underlying message is one of consolation: nothing is lost yet, if you would only act quickly. Although Bathsheba probably says nothing which is factually incorrect, her address at the same time consists of total and refined manipulation" (Fokkelman, *Narrative Art,* 357–58).

38. Ibid., 356.

Chapter 5

"Job and the Womb; Text about Men; Subtext about Women," in *A Feminist Companion to Wisdom Literature,* ed. Athalya Brenner, FCB 9 (Sheffield: Sheffield Academic, 1996), 186–200.

1. The words are also differentiated in Hebrew. *Yāšār,* "upright," "straightforward"; *ṣaddîq,* "righteous"; *tam,* "complete, with integrity."

2. Hayden White, "The Real, the True and the Figurative in the Human Sciences," *Profession* 92 (1992): 16.

3. Job has been subject to intense scrutiny; his wife has been, until recently, largely neglected. In detailed studies of the book, such as those by Robert Gordis, *The Book of God and Man: A Study of Job* (Chicago: University of Chicago Press, 1978), or N. H. Tur-Sinai, *The Book of Job: A New Commentary*

(Jerusalem: Kiryath Sepher, 1967), her words receive the mandatory commentary: she has only six words; the remarks are commensurately short. In less detailed analyses, she is often ignored. A respected collection of essays on Job includes one cursory mention of his wife in the entire book, although the servants and children of Job are elsewhere identified as "human beings as vital, as precious, as worthy of life . . . as Job himself" (P. Weiss, "God, Job and Evil," in *Dimensions of Job: A Study and Selected Readings,* ed. Nahum M. Glatzer [New York: Schocken, 1969], 183). It is an interesting oversight that Job's wife is not included among those worthy of life. Only recently has this disregarded woman drawn some attention. David Penchansky interprets "the story of Job's wife [as] a parable that carries the prescriptive message of the entire work" (*The Betrayal of God: Ideological Conflict in Job* [Louisville: Westminster John Knox, 1990], 85); and Ilana Pardes suggests that Job's wife "prefigures or perhaps generates the impatience of the dialogues" (*Countertraditions in the Bible: A Feminist Approach* [Cambridge, Mass.: Harvard Univ. Press, 1992], 147), which signals the beginning of Job's "growing interest in human relations" (52). Job's wife has been traditionally regarded as peripheral in the extreme, but is now becoming more noticeable.

4. Many of the books of the Prophets have no overt feminine voice, nor does Qoheleth among the Writings. By comparison, in the Book of Ruth, where female voices prevail, either Ruth or Naomi may dominate their mutual conversations; however, Ruth is typically brief and (metaphorically) direct before Boaz, who is comparatively more verbose.

5. Tur-Sinai, *The Book of Job,* lxii.

6. The ambiguity of *bārek* in this verse has drawn critical attention. Marvin H. Pope suggests that since cursing God does not necessarily lead to death, Job's wife tells him to at least "give vent to his feelings, or hers," in the little time he has left to live (*Job,* AB 15 [Garden City, N.Y.: Doubleday, 1983], 23). Edwin Good, reading 2:9 positively and negatively, offers several interpretations: as a farewell, as an encouragement, or as an expression of pity, positively; or as rebellion, negatively. He acknowledges that Job hears her words negatively (*In Turns of Tempest: A Reading of Job, with a Translation* [Stanford: Stanford Univ. Press, 1990], 200).

7. Indeed, he does not answer her question: he rebukes her for her words. All the other speakers' questions are rhetorical in that they do not seek to elicit information.

8. The Hebrew word *ha-n^ebālôth,* which I translate as "the wicked women," has also been translated as "foolish women," based on the root sequence *nbl,*

"senseless, foolish" (BDB, 615), but this translation fails to convey the immoral and disgraceful aspects implicit in the word. In Deuteronomy, the bride who is not a virgin is stoned to death because "she has wrought folly (*n^ebālāh*) in Israel" (Deut 22:21). Job does not call his wife "foolish," with its implications of "silly," but "wicked."

9. This is generally agreed upon. Pope translates the name as "dove" (*Job*, 348); Tur-Sinai as "little dove" (*Book of Job*, 581).

10. This translation is in response to a suggestion by Athalya Brenner. Pope translates *q^esî'āh* as "cinnamon" (*Job*, 348); Tur-Sinai identifies the noun "specifically as the peel of the aromatic plant *Laurus cassia*" (*The Book of Job*, 581).

11. My translation. Compare Pope: "Horn of Kohl" (*Job*, 348); Tur-Sinai: "flask of the blue paint with which women smeared their eyes" (*The Book of Job*, 581). Many commentaries disregard the daughters and the significance of their names altogether; for example, Gordis, *Book of God and Man*; Penchansky, *Betrayal of God*.

12. See above. This *hapax legomenon* is thought to be derived from an Aramaic word for "dove" (BDB, 410b). The more familiar word for "dove," *yônāh*, is not utilized in this text; and the metaphoric associations for *yônāh* cannot be assumed for *y^emîmāh*.

13. If the sound of the dove is the desired connotative image, the daughters' names make use of three sensory images—auditory, olfactory, and visual—to evoke a sensual response. This seems more plausible than Tur-Sinai's assessment that the daughters' names disclose a "tradition which no doubt gave further particulars of Job's family" (*Book of Job*, 582).

14. Pardes, *Countertraditions in the Bible*, 153.

15. Samson's name, *šimšôn*, echoing *šem*, "name," is as ironic as the fact that his observant, intelligent mother is unnamed while his skeptical, rather dense father (Manoah) is named. Compare Edward L. Greenstein, "The Riddle of Samson," *Prooftexts* 34 (1981): 237–60.

16. Moshe Greenberg, "Job," in *The Literary Guide to the Bible*, ed. Robert Alter and Frank Kermode (Cambridge: Harvard Univ. Press, 1987), 286.

17. The Adversary, who has two speeches, is also restricted to the narrative frame (the prologue, in fact). This is justified by his acting as a catalyst, no longer necessary once the action has been precipitated; and the Adversary is not a consistent object of textual breaks either in form or in language. See Athalya Brenner's discussion of the Adversary's function in "Job the Pious: The Characterization of Job in the Narrative Framework of the Book," *JSOT* 43 (1989): 37–52.

18. Churchmen have typically interpreted Job's wife as a temptress, and her words as a temptress's words. Pope notes that "Augustine called Job's wife *diaboli adjutrix* and Calvin, *organum Satanae*" (*Job*, 21–22n. 9).

19. The verbs *ḥpṣ* (delight in), *ksp* (long for), *'bh* (desire), *š'p* (desire), *ḥmd* (desire), *'wh* (desire, incline toward), *pth* (entice, seduce). Nouns in this connection are, for instance, *bṭn* (belly—the seat of desire) and *tqwh* (hope).

20. BDB, 107.

21. In Athalya Brenner and Fokkelein van Dijk-Hemmes, *On Gendering Texts: Female and Male Voices in the Hebrew Bible* (Leiden: Brill, 1993), 143.

22. Benjamin Davidson, *Analytical Hebrew and Chaldee Lexicon* (Peabody, Mass.: Hendrickson, 1984), 237.

23. BDB, 266.

24. Tur-Sinai, *The Book of Job*, 300.

25. God, in his reproach to Job, characterizes males as those who beget: "Has the rain a father, or who has begotten the drops of dew?" (36:28).

The male as begetter is not qualified in a synecdoche as a penis; in an adjoining verse, however, the female (the speaker is a presumably male God) is so imaged as a womb: "From whose womb did the ice come forth, and who has given birth to the hoarfrost of heaven?" (38:29). See also 38:8, discussed below.

26. However, sequences may begin with either word. It is worth noting that *bṭn/rḥm* occur in the Hebrew Bible as a parallel pair six times, three of which are in Job (3:11; 10:18-19; 31:15).

27. In other sections of the Hebrew Bible, *reḥem* may denote the organ of reproduction (Gen 25:23) or, more typically, birth (Judg 13:5; Ps 110:3).

28. This phrase is often emended; for example, "I am loathsome to the sons of my own mother" (RSV), or "I am loathsome to my own family" (RSV).

29. However, "sons" may refer to extended family (compare Deut 18:5; Judg 19:22). The meaning of the clause is not clear but the claiming of the womb, however oblique, is.

30. Robert Alter, *The Art of Biblical Poetry* (New York: Basic, 1985), 99.

Chapter 6

"Michal, the Barren Wife," in *A Feminist Companion to Samuel and Kings*, ed. Athalya Brenner. FCB 5 (Sheffield: Sheffield Academic, 1994), 37–46.

1. Daughters, such as Tamar, are mentioned only as they appear in narrative texts.

2. Biblical texts do not admit to the possibility of male infertility among Israelites.

3. Sarah is 90 years old when she first conceives (Gen 17:17).

4. Sarah (Gen 11:30) is forgotten, and Rachel is neglected in favor of Leah (Gen 29:31). Both women are later "remembered." Hannah (1 Sam 2:21) gains pregnancy by prayer.

5. Adele Berlin attributes the "notice that she loved David and that she made it known" to Michal's "unfeminine traits," and suggests that David "expresses more feelings of love and tenderness for the passive and submissive Jonathan than for the aggressive and physical Michal" ("Characterization in Biblical Narrative: David's Wives," in *Telling Queen Michal's Story: An Experiment in Comparative Interpretation,* ed. David J. A. Clines and Tamara C. Eskenazi, JSOTSup 119 (Sheffield: Sheffield Academic, 1991), 91–93. In view of David's developing history of relationships with women (e.g., Abigail, Bathsheba) and men (e.g., Nabor, Uriah), Berlin's focus on gender in these relationships seems unwarranted. David's preference is for individuals he can *control:* he apparently prefers docile women—and men—to independent and resourceful ones.

6. Peter D. Miscall, "Michal and her Sisters," in *Telling Queen Michal's Story,* 250.

7. Zafrira Ben-Barak, "The Legal Background to the Restoration of Michal to David," in *Telling Queen Michal's Story,* 86.

8. Danna Nolan Fewell and David M. Gunn, *Gender, Power and Promise: The Subject of the Bible's First Story* (Nashville: Abingdon, 1993), 157.

9. Ben-Barak has uncovered legal documentary material from Mesopotamia suggesting that when a husband is absent *against his will* for a period of two years, the wife—who is left without subsistence since she belongs to her husband's family—is declared a "widow" and is entitled to remarry. Should the first husband return, the woman is obliged to return to him, but any children remain with their natural father. David is forced to flee for his life *against his will,* and Ben-Barak suggests that Saul's action in giving Michal to another man as wife is to be regarded as "a customary official act and not as the arbitrary act of Saul giving his daughter in marriage" ("The Legal Background," 81–86, 88–89).

10. Emotional attachment is entirely discounted by R. K. Harrison: "The obvious attachment of Phaltiel to Michal, as recorded in 2 Samuel 3:16, is again understandable if she was in fact heiress to the throne, for in marrying her he would be in the direct line of succession" ("The Matriarchate and Hebrew Regal Succession," *EvQ* 29.1 [1957]: 29–34).

11. Although these musical instruments are explicitly mentioned only in the first phase of the journey, it is assumed that they also accompany the ark in

the second phase, from Obed-edom's house to the City of David, especially since David dances in the second phase.

12. This is the Septuagint reading. The Masoretic text reads "my own."

13. Excluding Palti as a husband, since that marriage was effectively annulled by her being returned to David, her first husband.

14. Robert Alter bemoans "modern translators [who] generally destroy the fineness of the effect of rendering the initial 'and' as 'so,'" thus establishing an unambiguous causal connection ("Characterization and the Art of Reticence," in *Telling Queen Michal's Story,* 73).

15. J. Cheryl Exum, "Murder They Wrote: Ideology and the Manipulation of Female Presence in Biblical Narrative," in Clines and Eskenazi, *Telling Queen Michal's Story,* 185.

16. Miscall, "Michal and her Sisters," 250n. 1.

17. Tamara C. Eskenazi, "Michal in Hebrew Sources," in Clines and Eskenazi, *Telling Queen Michal's Story,* 158.

18. Eskenazi, "Michal in Hebrew Sources," 159–74.

19. Ibid., 173.

Chapter 7

"Honor and Shame in Esther," in *A Feminist Companion to Esther, Judith and Susanna,* ed. Athalya Brenner. FCB 7 (Sheffield: Sheffield Academic, 1995), 149–175.

1. Sidnie A. White, "Esther: A Feminine Model for Jewish Diaspora," in *Gender and Difference in Ancient Israel,* ed. Peggy L. Day (Minneapolis: Fortress Press, 1989), 161–77.

2. Lyn M. Bechtel, "Shame as a Sanction of Social Control in Biblical Israel: Judicial, Political, and Social Shaming," *JSOT* 49 (1991): 63.

3. Compare the illumination of ancient anthropological artifacts through contemporary sociological fieldwork in Carol L. Meyers, "Everyday Life: Women in the Period of the Hebrew Bible," in *The Women's Bible Commentary,* ed. Carol A. Newsom and Sharon H. Ringe (Louisville: Westminster John Knox, 1992), 245. See also Carol Delaney, "Seeds of Honor, Fields of Shame," in *Honor and Shame and Unity of the Mediterranean,* ed. David D. Gilmore (Washington, D.C.: American Anthropological Association, 1987), 35–48; Bruce J. Malina, *The New Testament World: Insights from Cultural Anthropology,* rev. ed. (Louisville: Westminster John Knox, 1993).

4. Bechtel, "Shame as a Sanction of Social Control," 49.

5. Quoting Bechtel: "guilt relates to the *internalized, societal and parental prohibitions or boundaries* that cannot be transgressed (as opposed to the internalized goals and ideals [of shame]" (italics in original). "Guilt" is imposed from *within* (conscience) and reinforced by social pressure; "shame" arises predominantly from *external* pressure and is intensified by the internal apprehension of being shamed. "Being ashamed," which Bechtel does not distinguish, is a negative aspect of shame. The passive voice emphasizes its *external* origin. See Bechtel, "Shame as a Sanction of Social Control," 53.

6. Malina, *New Testament World*, 51.

7. Ibid., 49.

8. Lila Abu-Lughod, *Veiled Sentiments: Honor and Poetry in a Bedouin Society* (Berkeley: University of California Press, 1986).

9. Malina, *New Testament World*, 54.

10. Ibid.

11. Bechtel, "Shame as a Sanction of Social Control," 66.

12. The king is the only character who bridges both actions.

13. Wesley J. Fuerst, *The Books of Ruth, Esther, Ecclesiastes, the Song of Songs, Lamentations: The Five Scrolls*, CBC (Cambridge: Cambridge Univ. Press, 1975), 44.

14. Malina, *New Testament World*, 45.

15. Marvin Harris, *Cannibals and Kings: The Origins of Cultures* (New York: Vintage, 1978), 113.

16. Persian drinking celebrations are historically verified; nevertheless, the narrative renders ironic the redistribution not of nourishing food but of alcohol, which, when consumed in the excessive quantities associated with Persian banquets, is detrimental to life.

17. I disagree with David J. A. Clines's claim that "on every other front [except the battle of the sexes] he [Ahasuerus] is masterfully supreme" (*The Esther Scroll: The Story of the Story*, JSOTSup 30 [Sheffield: JSOT Press, 1984], 32).

18. According to Israel Bettan, a midrash explains that the king issues an order allowing the guests to drink at their own discretion. "On festive occasions the Persian rulers used to serve wine in large cups which guests were duty-bound to drain." This time they were not so constrained (*The Five Scrolls: A Commentary on the Song of Songs, Ruth, Lamentations, Ecclesiastes, Esther* [Cincinnati: Union of American Hebrew Congregations, 1950], 205). See also George M. Lamsa, *Old Testament Light: The Indispensable Guide to the Customs, Manners, and Idioms of Biblical Times* (San Francisco: Harper & Row, 1964), 404. The midrash makes it seem that the king is protecting his guests from

overindulgence. This is not supported by the statement that the king's "heart was merry with wine" (1:10). Surely his guests drank as he did. Michael V. Fox has a clearer analysis: "The point is that no one was forced to drink, but that no one was kept from drinking when and as much as he wished, and that *this* was the king's 'law' or edict: to let everyone do as he wished" (italics in original) (*Character and Ideology in the Book of Esther* [Columbia: University of South Carolina Press, 1991], 17). In any case, the control of drinking is shifted from the king to the guests.

19. This pattern of elevation and denigration initially includes Haman as part of the Persian court, but Haman will be distinguished from the Persians.

20. This is virtually the only specific command the king initiates on his own; and it is impulsive, shortsighted and probably drunken. All other such royal commands follow the advice of others—servants, court advisors and even a woman, his queen—until the conclusion.

21. E. J. Bickerman, *Four Strange Books of the Bible: Jonah, Daniel, Koheleth, and Esther* (New York: Schocken, 1967), 185–86.

22. *Esther Rabbah* 3.13-14 (trans. M. Simon; London: Soncino, 1951).

23. Clines, *Esther Scroll,* 32.

24. Modern beauty contests expose as much of the body as is socially acceptable. Of course, a king can establish his own rules of exposure.

25. A beauty contest demands greater than normal exposure, especially in a society that demands that its women be covered and veiled. Even uncovering of the face is "exposure," though more disrobing is presumed in a beauty contest. Nakedness is not.

26. Abu-Lughod, *Veiled Sentiments,* 152–53.

27. The sexual bond is threatening to the kinship bond: it can break up male-determined kinship lines. To counter this, females are conditioned to remain primarily loyal to patrilineal kin (ibid., 148–49).

28. Fox proposes that "the actual competition, to take place after a year of beauty treatments, is a *sex* contest, with the winner being whoever can most please the king during her night with him" (italics in original) (*Character and Ideology,* 28).

29. White suggests that the reader "accept the worldview of the text" that makes Esther "a more sympathetic character." Honor/shame helps interpret that worldview ("Esther," 168).

30. It also hints that although he dictates laws and commandments, the king does no reading or writing on his own, further poking fun at his autonomy.

31. See 1 Sam 15; 27:8; 30:1, 18; 2 Sam 1:1; 1 Chron 4:43.

32. "'Worship' originally meant "worthiness," "a recognition of worth" (Malina, *The New Testament World*, 48).

33. As in Exod 17:8-16, esp. 16b: "for үнwн wages war against the Amalekites generation after generation."

34. Haman is here specifically identified as an enemy of the Jews (3:10).

35. Without insight into honor/shame, R. Lubitch questions "How narrow-minded could [Esther] possibly have been to send clothes for Mordekhai before investigating the matter!" ("A Feminist's Look at Esther," *Judaism* 42 [1993]: 440).

36. "Normally [fasting] involved abstinence from all food to show dependence on God and submission to his will" (J. N. Suggit, "Fasting," in *The Oxford Companion to the Bible*, ed. Bruce M. Metzger and Michael D. Coogan [New York: Oxford Univ. Press, 1993], 225).

37. This also accords with her participation in the Persian beauty contest and its sexual consequences.

38. Both men are invited, but the banquet is prepared for the king.

39. It also reverses Vashti's nonappearance in a male space by inviting Haman to a female space.

40. Bechtel, "Shame as a Sanction of Social Control," 61.

41. Malina, *New Testament World*, 67.

42. See Sandra Beth Berg's cogent analysis of Haman's petition to Ahasuerus and Esther's response in her plea in *The Book of Esther: Motifs, Themes, and Structure*, SBL Dissertation Series 44 (Missoula, Mont.: Scholars Press, 1979), 100–103.

43. In the Hebrew of 7:9, the last sentence may be understood as "his face was covered" (but compare suggestions in *BHS* to emend, following the LXX). The "covering" of Haman's face, however, is *not* in preparation for the gallows (as our knowledge of European custom might tempt us to assume). In any event, the king has no knowledge of the already-prepared "tree" until he is informed by Harbona the eunuch in the next verse (7:10).

44. Autonomy is closely identified with sexual prowess, and a slight to a male's honor implies a slight to his sexual competence.

45. Her presence does raise the question of the danger involved in an unsummoned appearance. The verse (8:3) begins, "Esther added and spoke before the king," which conveys the impression that her comments occurred at the same sitting. It may be that Esther was present when Mordecai was honored and that she uses the opportunity to introduce her own interests. To counter this assumption, the text also says, "the king held out the golden scepter toward

Esther" (8:4), suggesting a separate appearance. Bettan says that the king's holding out his scepter is not a sign of audience but of favor to her petition (*The Five Scrolls*, 236).

46. "Honor might be described as socially proper attitudes and behavior in the area where the three lines of power, gender status and religion intersect" (Malina, *New Testament World*, 31).

47. Their refusal "reverses" the sin of the Israelite war with the Amalekites (1 Samuel 15), when Saul disobeyed by allowing the people to take booty.

48. Nevertheless, there must have been some segment that thought as Haman did if the numbers of people killed by the Jews (9:5-6, 16) are indicative of an opposition.

49. Contrary to all the drinking parties of the Persians, no drink is mentioned here. Nevertheless, Purim traditionally includes plenty of drinking.

50. This phrase may also be translated "and pleasing to many of his kinsmen," implying a veiled criticism of Mordecai.

Scripture Index

Subject and Author Index